It allows a homebuyer to decrease their interest rate by 1% in year one. The borrower will reach the full monthly payment in year two.

Are you ready to be a homeowner?
Contact us today to learn more!

DHI MORTGAGE
A D.R. Horton® Company
www.dhimortgage.com

Ethan Neff NMLS / License # MLO-281957
Branch Manager

4380 SW Macadam Ave., Suite 100
Portland, OR 97239
EHNeff@dhimortgage.com

Direct: 503-721-2370
Cell: 503-348-1424
Efax: 800-779-1344
www.dhimortgage.com/ethan-ne

D1577930

THE 4:2 FORMULA

GETTING BUYERS OFF THE FENCE
AND INTO A HOME

BY JEFF SHORE

ISBN: 978-0-9884915-0-2

Printed by Data Reproductions Corporation

Auburn Hills, MI

Cover design by Vanessa Maynard

Marketing Director: Cassandra Grauer (cassandra@jeffshore.com)

Contents

The 4:2 Formula: Getting Started vii

SECTION 1

1. Why Do People Move? 1
2. Understanding Dissatisfaction 7
3. Types and Degrees of Dissatisfaction 13
4. The Power of "Why?" 19
5. The Why Behind the "Why?" 25
6. Boldness in Questioning 31

SECTION 2

7. Motivation Factor #1: Current Dissatisfaction 35
8. Motivation Factor #2: Future Promise 43
9. Inhibitor Factor #1: Cost 51
10. Inhibitor Factor #2: Fear 57
11. The Buying Formula 63

SECTION 3

12. Standardized Scripting vs. Strategic Structure 75

13. Why vs. What 81

14. The 4:2 Formula 85

15. Discovery Category #1: Trust Building 89

16. Discovery Category #2: Motivation Questions 99

17. Discovery Category #3: Current Dissatisfaction 105

18. Discovery Category #4: Future Promise 111

19. The Summary Questions 117

20. Summary Question #1: The Summary Dissatisfaction Question (SDQ) 121

21. Summary Question #2: The Summary Solution Question (SSQ) 125

22. Filling In the Information Gaps 129

SECTION 4

The 10-Week Study Guide to 4:2 Selling 133

Let's Get To Work 135

Appendix 1: Success Stories 157

Appendix 2: Sample Scripts 165

Dedication

To the sales professionals who make real estate
the greatest industry on the planet.

The 4:2 Formula: Getting Started

I'd like to make a slightly preposterous claim: if you know your clients well enough, they will show you how to sell them a home. I believe this because I've seen it work over and over again, all around the world.

I also suggest that one of the biggest problems salespeople face is having been taught an approach that centers on the product rather than on the prospect. All too often, the sales presentation is nothing more than a massive assault of features and benefits. It's as if the salesperson is saying, "Open wide while I jam this down your throat. Then you can tell me if you like the taste."

At the core of this issue is a lack of understanding about why our clients are standing in front of us in the first place. We'll dive into that issue in this book. Sure, we want to know how to lure prospects off the fence, but shouldn't we first want to know what got them on the fence in the first place? We'll tackle that one as well. As salespeople, we want to get to the specifics of the home search, but we stop short of understanding why those specifics *mean* something to a particular buyer. Yep, that's on the list as well.

In the pages that follow, I'd like to help you understand your clients at a level you've never thought possible. In doing so, I'll show you how to establish a sense of mutual purpose—a connection that puts you shoulder to shoulder with your client as you walk down the sales path. In the process, I'd like to help you become that Trusted Advisor you aspire to be.

Now, let me say what you *won't* find in this book.

First, you won't find pages and pages of scripts to memorize. Yes, there are samples of phrasings, but I leave it up to you to find and use your own sales voice.

Second, you won't find a lot of outrageous and unusable sales lines. I believe that salespeople serve through *leading* their clients, not through *manipulating* them.

Third, you won't find a lot of stories about the way the author used to do things in 1985. This book is relevant and timely for today; its principles are being applied all over the world.

Fourth and finally, you won't find the "same old thing" in these pages. Instead, you'll discover a unique approach to getting to know your clients on a deep level. You'll also notice a stark absence of questions like these: "How many bedrooms are you looking for?"; "What brought you out today?"; "How soon are you thinking about moving?" and "What's your price range?"

So my role in writing this book is to bring you fresh new concepts that can completely revolutionize your sales process. You have a part as well, and it begins with *active reading*. That's why I encourage you—I *beg* you—to read each chapter with a pen, notebook, and highlighter. Stop frequently and jot down your thoughts or highlight key concepts. Write out phrasing for your own sales language. Challenge yourself to practice out loud as you go along (unless you're reading this book at the library!).

To support that, you'll find Application Breaks throughout the book. They are tips and ideas you can use repeatedly. That way, you aren't only gaining an intellectual understanding; you're also honing specific skills. Plus you will find Study Questions at the end of each chapter. Don't skip over these! They'll help you apply what you're learning as you go.

I *know* you can get a great deal out of the concepts that follow. But this book wasn't written for you to get something out of it; it was written to get something out of you—*your very best sales presentation!*

Let's do it. Let's go change someone's world!

SECTION 1:

THE CLIENTS' MISSION

Chapter One:
Why Do People Move?

What is the single most motivating factor in a home-buying decision?

Think about your typical clients for a moment. Maybe they are young couples just buying their first home, ready to start a family and live the American dream. They've spent the past few years moving from one crappy apartment to the next as they get their careers off the ground. Now, they're looking for the perfect home.

> *"I am one of those people who thrive on deadlines. Nothing brings on inspiration more readily than desperation."*
>
> **Harry Shearer**

Or perhaps your typical clients are middle-aged couples. They've recently sent the last of their brood off to college and have suddenly realized the family home is too big for just two. Besides, they want to live closer to the city where the action is. They would love to have a luxury condo as a base camp for their upcoming travels and adventures.

Perhaps it's the multi-generational family moving in together. Or the single woman, career-minded and driven. Or the relocation buyer moving from out of state to your city.

So, what do these clients have in common?

Probably your instinctive answer is that they're looking for the perfect home. Or perhaps you think it is convenience, good neighborhood, great location, or the alluring features and amenities a home has to offer. Maybe you suggest that they're seeking the home of their dreams and once they see it, they'll fall in love with it and just have to buy it. And of course, everyone will live happily ever after, right? But that isn't the question.

Again, the real question is "what is the single most motivating factor in a home-buying decision?"

The fact is this: location, convenience, neighborhood, and even the features of a home are all things that might cause a client to buy one home over the other. But that's not the single most motivating factor in a home-buying decision. It goes much deeper.

Take a moment to get into your client's head on this one. Go ahead, I'll wait . . .

Do you know what that single most motivating factor is yet? In a word: Dissatisfaction.

That's probably not what you expected to hear, but if you understand this as part of the homebuyer's mindset, you will have a significant leg up on your competitors. You will learn things about your clients that most salespeople will never know. And the sale will roll out right in front of you.

Let's explore this idea in more depth.

Think about the home *you* are living in right now. Then rate your Dissatisfaction with that home. On a scale of 1 to 10, with 1 meaning that you are very happy with the home, the neighborhood, and so on. It's your dream home, and you wouldn't even think about living anywhere else.

At the other end of the scale, a rating of 10 means you are highly dissatisfied; perhaps the neighborhood has been in steady decline, the basement floods with the slightest bit of rain, the neighbors play polka music at ungodly hours, and you just can't bear to stay another night in the place!

Where does your home rate on the scale?

Let's assume you are in the majority, which is 4 or below. You are fairly satisfied and have very few issues, if any at all, about your current living situation. It would be safe to say your discontent level is low. So, how would your home search be coming along right now? You would be actively looking, wouldn't you? No?

Of course not! You see, people who have little Dissatisfaction with their homes are not in the market. In fact, they aren't even lookers. I could show that kind of client the nicest, most tricked-out home in town. It's got granite countertops, stainless steel appliances, and brushed nickel fixtures. It's been decked out by one of the top designers

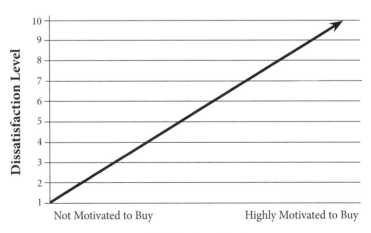

Dissatisfaction - Motivation Relationship

in town; it's located in a gated community with just the sweetest neighbors I could find . . . all at a 10% discount. Sounds like a winner, right?

But if you're 100% satisfied with the home you live in now, *all those things don't matter.*

I contend that the single most motivating factor in buying a home is Dissatisfaction. It also happens to be one of the most under-discovered aspects of the selling process.

Application Break

- Take time right now to evaluate your opening questions. Think about what you typically ask your clients when you first meet—that is, after you say "hello" but before you start talking about what you'd like to show them.

- Do those early questions lead you to a deep sense of what is wrong with their lives, with how their lives need to be improved? Do the questions address more about what the client is moving toward, or more about what he/she is moving away from?

- Be thinking about the questions you could be asking to determine that sense of Dissatisfaction.

DISMANTLING THE CRITICAL PATH

If you've been in the real estate industry for any length of time, you've probably come across this "Critical Path" sales method: greet, qualify, demonstrate, close. It seems as if every sales guru in the real estate industry has a variation of the Critical Path method—one that's guaranteed to make you a top producer.

If only it were that easy! I'm here to refute that method. I'm simply not a Critical Path guy . . . never have been and never will be.

You see, your clients don't operate in a vacuum. They can't be fenced in by a method that doesn't allow for one of the most important factors of selling: that you're dealing with human beings *who operate on emotion.* The problem with the Critical Path method is that it's both linear and overly simplistic. More important, it's about how the seller wants to sell.

Let's talk instead about *how the buyer wants to buy.*

Sure, you can greet your clients, find out how much house they can afford, and proceed to show them home after home after home. The Critical Path spends too much time focusing on the manner in which the seller will sell, how long it will take them to do so, and how close they can get to their asking price. At that rate, you'll be spinning your wheels trying to get those clients to make a purchase decision. That is if they don't just jump ship before then and find someone who actually understands them!

So, let's not concern ourselves with methods designed to help the seller sell right now. When dealing with homebuyers, I'm far more interested in how the buyers will buy and what drives their choice. What motivates people to pull the trigger and happily sign on the dotted line?

In fact, I'll go even further with what might be a provocative statement to you: "If you know your clients well enough, they will show you how to sell them a home. If you truly understand them on a deep enough level, the sales path should roll right out in front of you."

And believe me; it will. At that point, your clients will roll out the red carpet of their innermost hopes, Fears, and dreams. However, being able to reach this point requires a greater sense of partnership than ever. And *that* re-

> *Winning Thought:*
> *Let the sales path appear as you get to know the customer's deepest motivations.*

quires a lot of trust and a deep sense of insight into the Dissatisfaction they're feeling.

STUDY QUESTIONS:

1. What did you learn about why people move?

2. What is the single most motivating factor in a home-buying decision?

3. What was your personal motivating factor in your last home-buying decision? How did this tie to Dissatisfaction?

4. The "Critical Path" sales method says "greet, qualify, demonstrate, close." Why is this approach ineffective in selling a house?

5. Why is it so important to understand *why* an individual homebuyer wants to buy?

Chapter Two:
Understanding Dissatisfaction

During her junior year of college, my daughter Katie came home for Mother's Day weekend, driving 400 miles from Southern to Northern California. Katie's glamorous ride was actually my old pickup truck that I lent her to have at school.

> *The "why" is far more important than the "what."*

At nine o'clock in the evening on the Thursday before Mother's Day, she called me on her cell phone from a loud place; that turned out to be the shoulder of Interstate 80. My truck had simply stopped running. Please understand the context: This is not a call a father likes to receive. I didn't like the idea of Katie being stranded like that.

We had the truck towed to our mechanic who called me Friday afternoon to officially pronounce the old pickup—in mechanical terms—dead. A blown head gasket had torn apart the radiator, which damaged one thing and then the other thing . . . you get the picture.

That call came in late on Friday. Katie was leaving for Southern California after church on Sunday. First question: what did our Saturday plans now consist of? If your answer is "car *shopping*," you would be wrong. We were not car shopping; we were car *buying*!

Next question: how important was my little story for the salesperson at the car dealership? One would think it to be critical. Yet we went to three different dealerships and not one salesperson figured it out. No one asked about need. What do you think they wanted to talk about? You got it—prices. Terms. Discounts. Incentives.

> *Ignore the Dissatisfaction and you will frustrate the entire sales process.*

As you can see, Dissatisfaction can be a powerful motivator. Without it, we might be tempted to put off what *must* get done. Dissatisfaction provides us with the desire to change our situation. *This is as true in life as it is in sales.* Have you ever been so hungry that you've surprised yourself with what you were willing to eat?

Say you have a big meeting at work and decide to skip lunch one day. You might feel a bit hungry, but it really isn't a pressing matter, and you're able to hold off until dinner with no sweat. Imagine though, that you have gone 24 hours without food. The urgency to eat becomes stronger and, instead of reaching for your usual healthy meal, you pull into a drive-through and get the greasiest burger they sell. Probably not the best option, but hey—you were hungry.

Now, imagine yourself out in the wilderness. You haven't eaten in four days. You're lightheaded, irritable, sluggish, and your stomach feels like it's eating itself. You see a cicada latched onto a tree, and suddenly something you never thought you would eat looks incredibly scrumptious. You are ravished, so you pick it off and eat it. At this point, you'll do anything to quell the ache in your empty stomach.

In this situation, your hunger acts as a motivator for change, and you'll do anything to make that change happen and the hunger feelings go away. You'll even do things you may not have considered before.

That's Dissatisfaction.

I once saw a woman walk into the men's room at the intermission of a concert and say, "Sorry, fellas, the line to the women's room is too long and I just can't wait."

Again, Dissatisfaction.

In the decision to move, there is no more powerful factor than Dissatisfaction. But wait—it gets better because not only does Dissatisfaction prove to be a powerful motivator, Dissatisfaction is also the driving force behind urgency. Just like the urgency experienced by the person who hasn't eaten in days or the woman who used the men's room because the line to the ladies' room was too long, clients who are dissatisfied with their home have that same emotional thought pattern. They need to move *and* they needed to make it to happen yesterday.

> *Dissatisfaction is the driving force behind urgency.*

If you can answer the call of their urgent pleas, you will be their hero.

In my work with real estate companies around the world, I'm constantly hit with the same question: "How come we can't get these buyers off the fence?" That's a good question, but I have a better one: "What got them on the fence in the first place?"

Figure out what got them on the fence, and you'll figure out how to get them off the fence. If you've ever wondered what makes homebuyers get off the fence, start with their Dissatisfaction.

Application Break

- In your typical discovery process, how soon do you determine what got your clients on the fence? Do you learn it in the first few minutes, or does it seem to take significantly longer than that?

- By now, you should be thinking about questions you could ask that would give you a deeper understanding of the clients' Dissatisfaction. Now begin to think about how to ask those questions early in the conversation. The sooner you know their pain, the sooner you can provide relief for it.

I don't suppose I'll ever become famous for this quote, but let me give it a try. *"The greatest motivation to buy new shoes is when you notice your sock is wet."*

No? Not exactly Covey-esque, is it? But the principle behind it is critically important.

It happened to me on a business trip to Chicago in January. I noticed my foot felt squishy, so I looked at the sole of my shoe and sure enough, a hole. Because I was on day two of a five-day trip, I had no choice; I had to buy a new pair of shoes.

Interestingly—and at a measure of surprise to me—I ended up buying the most expensive pair of shoes I have ever owned. The salesperson at Nordstrom already knew I needed to buy a pair of shoes; that was a given. But in his questioning, he discovered several things about me:

1. I am on my feet all day long; comfort is critical.
2. I want to project an image of success; cheap doesn't work.

3. I wear a lot of suits; an upscale oxford lace-up makes sense.

4. I am constantly going through security at airports; it's a pain when it comes to removing my shoes.

He proceeded to show me a shoe that was stunningly classy and exceedingly comfortable. It had a hidden elastic in the side so it had the elegance of a lace-up but performed like a loafer—I could easily slip it on and off at an airport security line.

Only after I was absolutely sold did he share with me the price. *Did you catch that?* Only after I was absolutely sold did he share with me the price. When the Dissatisfaction is high enough, and the Future Promise is great enough, the Cost is practically a non-issue. Had he led the discussion with "What is your price range?" I would have purchased the wrong shoes!

If you remember nothing else from this book, remember this: *the single greatest force in a homebuyer's urgency is Dissatisfaction.* This is because Dissatisfaction causes us to feel uncomfortable, which creates the urgency and motivation to remove the source of that discomfort. The longer we go without being able to remove the discomfort and get back to a positive state of being, the more urgent our situation becomes. Sometimes, the urgency gets to the point of being willing to make pretty serious sacrifices to achieve a state of satisfaction once again.

So it can be said that the higher the degree of Dissatisfaction the homebuyers have, the higher their urgency is. Conversely, the lower the Dissatisfaction they have, the less urgency they will have to make a change, if at all. That being said, there are different degrees or categories we can put this Dissatisfaction into.

Let's take a look at that.

STUDY QUESTIONS:

1. Think back to a time you had your own "squishy foot" experience and had to buy something urgently. What was it? How did you decide what to buy? How did you feel about your decision?

2. How can you use personal understanding to help you look for urgency factors from your clients *and* help them be ready to make a decision to buy?

3. Do you have the patience to spend time understanding your clients' Current Dissatisfaction? If not, what can you do to increase your patience?

4. Think about your last two or three home-buying clients. List some of their underlying needs—ones that would help them be sold on a property *before* you bring up price.

Chapter Three:
Types and Degrees
of Dissatisfaction

Dissatisfaction comes in many forms; there are numerous reasons why homebuyers might feel the urgency to move. At times, that Dissatisfaction might be tied to the home itself, but it could also be about other things. For some homebuyers, it might concern a life change such as a new job, getting married, or having a baby. All of these life changes can cause homebuyers to assess whether their current home is meeting all of their needs. If it isn't, they'll likely become dissatisfied and feel the need to find something more suitable.

> *"He who has a why to live can bear almost any how."*
>
> **Nietzsche**

So, what pushes those clients over the edge and makes them say, "This is it! I'm not putting up with this leaky roof, polka-playing neighbors, and downtrodden neighborhood. It's time to move on and find something better!"

Think about it for a moment. Why couldn't they stay where they were and just, you know, make it work? What was it about their lives that needed to improve?

In some cases, the answer is simple. Maybe one of them got a new job or a promotion out of state. Maybe they had the perfect home in the perfect neighborhood, close to everything, and the kids loved it. But add job relocation to the mix and no matter how perfect the home in every way, they can't take it with them to a new town. These clients have become dissatisfied and now feel a strong sense of urgency to find a suitable place to live in that new town.

Or, let's take someone newly divorced. (I actually like the term "domestic restructure"—it's more pleasant.) His or her Dissatisfaction stems from the recent life change, not the home. Although he or she may have been perfectly happy with the current structure, the new single status demands a change of residence—whether it be to downsize, follow a dream, or forget the past. The urgency to move is now in play.

What about empty nesters? Again, their house didn't change; their lives did. They may no longer have a need for a large home with lots of bedrooms. Or maybe they want to pursue their dreams of retiring to the mountains, the ocean, or the city. As their children went off to college and began their own lives, the empty nesters' needs—and thus their relationship with their home—changed.

And sometimes people just fall out of love. It happens in relationships more often than most of us like to admit, and it happens with our homes even more frequently. It's that old case of "Well, it felt right at the time, so we did it!"

For many homebuyers, their current home may well have been just right for them at some point. But they're over it now . . . like a stale relationship with no spark. It could be the design or the dated décor or the lack of energy efficiency. It might just be boredom and the desire to find someplace new. Either way, Dissatisfaction has set in and a growing sense of urgency is finding its way into these homebuyers' hearts.

In all of these cases, Dissatisfaction is the motivating factor when it comes to why people move.

DISSATISFACTION OVER TIME

After thinking about different reasons people have for becoming dissatisfied, you may have realized that it isn't a kind of static emotion that doesn't go anywhere. In fact, you may have noticed from your own personal experiences that Dissatisfaction tends to grow over time. It's dynamic; once it starts, it can easily take on a life of its own.

As a rule, your home does not change as dramatically as your life. Over the last five-year period, did your home or your neighborhood change all that much? Not really. But what about your life—does your life change over five years? You bet. Notice how our lives change *apart* from our homes. I call this the "Dissatisfaction gap." The Dissatisfaction gap grows over time as your life moves you away from your home.

The Dissatisfaction Gap

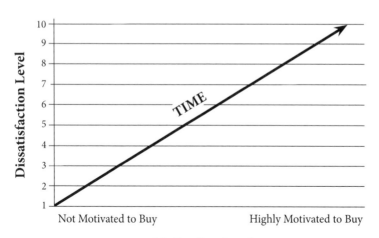

The Dissatisfaction gap is real, but many homebuyers either don't realize it or don't want to share it. Homebuyers don't want salespeople to know just how much Dissatisfaction they feel and how urgent their need really is. Think about it. Have you ever heard a homebuyer say, "Oh, well we just started looking" or "We're not in a rush; we want to make sure we find the perfect place"? These statements are usually made in a feeble attempt to convince the seller they won't be buying soon. Nope, no desperation, no sense of urgency there—everything's *juuuust* fine.

Maybe . . . maybe not.

Suppose two clients come to your open house and tell you they've been in the market for four weeks. As a curious sales professional, you ask them why they're thinking about moving and they reply "Oh, well our house is too small."

Now, what just happened . . .

No, wait. Think about what did *not* happen . . .

There's absolutely no way one of those people rolled out of bed that morning, walked into the kitchen, took a look around, and stated, "Say—this kitchen is too small! Now, how did that happen?" The fact is, that kitchen has been "too small" for a long time. And that means that person has been in the market for years!

Still not convinced? Stay with me here.

Think about the trend over the past five years. Are people staying in their homes for longer periods or shorter? Staying put longer. This trend is increasing year after year. That means there's no longer a Dissatisfaction, right?

Wrong! In fact, what it means is that their Dissatisfaction is *higher* than ever. We live in a time when many homeowners want to move but don't have the means to. They're highly dissatisfied with their current digs but may not be able to do anything about it. It will take an extremely high degree of Dissatisfaction and urgency to get that home-owner to budge.

Application Break

- Think about the last three prospects you have worked with, whether they purchased from you or not. What likely drove them crazy in the home they lived in (or are still living in)? Frame that answer in emotional terms.

- For example, does your understanding stop at "Their current home is too small"? Or can you say, "They've got three growing children who are constantly bickering over sharing bedrooms. The tension in that house seems to be thick."

Let's go back to the wondrous days of 2005 . . .

How dissatisfied did homeowners have to be with their homes before they broke down and put them on the market? If you were there, you would know it didn't take much: "Oh look, honey, the counter tile is chipped. Let's sell. What did the neighbor get for his house? We'll add $20,000." That was the norm for many sellers at that point. A low threshold for Dissatisfaction created an unrealistic sense of urgency that had people selling their homes left and right in an attempt to find the next best thing.

But that's not true with the way the economy has been the past few years. Now, people are living with their Dissatisfaction for long periods—not to mention they're learning to adjust to it. It takes serious Dissatisfaction to get today's homeowners to budge. They're learning to live with it—until they can't stand it anymore, that is.

That's when they show up in your office.

So, are you convinced yet?

You should be, because if you don't understand the depth of your clients' Dissatisfaction, you're in for a rough ride. Understand that Dissatisfaction and you'll be a hero; miss it and you'll be facing a difficult sale—or maybe no sale at all.

STUDY QUESTIONS:

1. How do you probe for home Dissatisfaction without being intrusive?

2. Is it only *unhappy* circumstances that bring about home Dissatisfaction? If not, how can a happy circumstance trigger home Dissatisfaction?

3. How would you monitor a client's Dissatisfaction over time? Could you actually graph it?

4. Some people are dissatisfied with their homes but haven't yet reached a high enough level of Dissatisfaction to do something about it. How could you keep track of these prospective clients who are in the market—even though they don't realize it yet?

Chapter Four:
The Power of "Why?"

So, you're probably thinking all you have to do is pinpoint your clients' Dissatisfaction and you'll be home free. Sounds easy, right? Well, there's just one little, itty, bitty, teensy problem.

> *"It is a miracle that curiosity survives formal education."*
>
> **Einstein**

Your clients don't come in wearing their Dissatisfaction on their sleeves. I mean, it's not like they just walk into your office with big scowls on their faces, lips twisted in disgust, and unload their problems on you. No, they don't *want* you to know how dissatisfied they are because they don't want to come off as desperate, needy, or worse, failures.

Until they trust you, the Dissatisfaction they feel is strictly personal, not something to be discussed with a real estate salesperson. As far as you're concerned, they're happy to give you one of their standard lines such as "we're looking for a home in a good school district for the kids" or "we just want to downsize."

You see, *trust* is the key that unlocks the door to understanding their Dissatisfaction.

A salesperson in Florida shared with me a powerful example. She had met an older gentleman at an open house and they had this conversation:

Salesperson:	*"What has you in the market for a home?"*
Client:	*"I'm downsizing."*
Salesperson:	*"Tell me more about that. Why the need to downsize at this point?"*
Client:	*"Well, it's just me. And, well, I dunno—I feel like I'm kicking around in my own house. It just doesn't work for me anymore."*
Salesperson:	*"I don't want to be nosy—I just want to understand. Did something change in your life?"*

At this point, the gentleman looked very uncomfortable, even pained. He paused and then said, *"Well, my wife passed. Six months ago. And now, every time I turn a corner in that house, it's painful. I thought I was going to stay there forever, but I'm just miserable."*

Let me ask you a question, sales professional. How much do you think this guy wanted to share that story when he first walked through the door? Not much, right? But how much did he absolutely *need* someone to talk to, someone who understood, someone who cared? I would say a great deal.

This leads me to one of the most overlooked and underdeveloped traits of a successful salesperson in home sales. Well, in all sales really. It's **the trait of deep curiosity.**

Have you ever known an insanely curious salesperson?

I bet you have. In fact, you may have one of them in your office right now. You know, that man or woman who just has to know exactly what makes his or her clients tick. He probes his clients tirelessly for information and knows exactly the right questions to ask. She excels at building trust and her clients feel comfortable opening up. There's no shame in their game, and they won't rest until they fully understand the depth of their clients' Dissatisfaction.

Alas, most salespeople are asking all the wrong questions from the start.

To get to the depth of any client's Dissatisfaction, you have to take a whole new perspective on the discovery process. Most salespeople focus on the superficial, the surface problems: "Oh, you say your house is too big/too small" or "So, you are looking for a good school district." These surface problems are simply effects of the larger issues at hand, the root of the clients' Dissatisfaction.

> *Curiosity is one of the most under-developed but incredibly powerful skill sets for sales professionals. And like any skill, it can be developed with focus and practice. Nurture a profound sense of curiosity and the sale will roll out in front of you!*

By focusing on the surface problems, you only get half of the story. At this point, making a sale is a crapshoot; you might make it a slam-dunk or completely miss your clients' point.

When getting to know prospective clients, focus on the root of their Dissatisfaction above all else. So, how do you do this?

Well, don't be like most salespeople who are stuck on these "what" questions:

- *"What size home are you looking for?"*
- *"What is your time frame?"*

- *"What is your price range?"*
- *"What is important to you in your new home?"*

These aren't *bad* questions; they certainly have a time and place. But a salesperson can ask all of these questions and still not understand the root of the clients' Dissatisfaction.

During a break in a training session, a brand new salesperson asked me, "In your opinion, what is the most important question to ask in all home sales?"

He was probably guessing I'd say any number of closing questions such as:

- *"Would you like to buy this home?"*
- *"How would you like to make it yours?"*
- *"What's it going to take to get you to make a decision today?"*

Did I respond with any of those? No, none of the above. In fact, I didn't even have to pause or hesitate with my answer. Do you know what the single most important question I ask all of my clients is, the question that gets to the root of their Dissatisfaction?

> *The single most important question in homes sales is: "Why are you thinking it's time to move?"*

One. Simple. Question. That's all it takes. It's all about the "why." Make that your mantra: "It's all about the why." If you don't know the "why," then the "what" really doesn't matter.

Application Break

- What is the most natural way for you to ask the one simple Motivation Question—the "why are you thinking about moving?" question? The only way to confirm what's natural to you is by practicing—out loud! I cannot stress this enough. You can't improve your performance by reading a book or attending a training session; it requires practicing *out loud*.

- Try it now. Put this book down and test how you would ask the question. What is the most natural delivery? What are the right word choices and inflections? Practice this question until it's second nature to you.

STUDY QUESTIONS:

1. How will you build trust with your homebuyers so they're willing to share personal stories with you?

2. What is the first question you can ask to determine a client's reason for Dissatisfaction?

3. What is the difference between saying "Do you want to buy a new house?" and saying "Tell me more about why you want to buy a new house"? How will your client respond to each of these?

Chapter Five:
The Why Behind the "Why?"

But, we can't stop there because the real issues are rarely found at the surface level. Think again about that one person in your office who always seems to "get" the clients. If he were to stop with one question, he'd probably only get a partial answer. Instead, he keeps probing until he finds out the *real* reason, the emotional trigger that's causing their Dissatisfaction.

Until we understand the clients' Dissatisfaction *from an emotional level,* our job is only half done.

> *"People understand me so poorly that they don't even understand my complaint about them not understanding me."*
>
> **Soren Kierkegaard**

Let's see this in a case study. A gentleman meets a salesperson who proceeds to ask, "Why are you thinking it might be time to move?"

The prospect replies, "Our home is too small."

Where might the conversation go now? If typical, we would see something like this.

Salesperson:	*"Oh, how big is your home?"*
Client:	*"Fifteen hundred square feet, three bedrooms."*
Salesperson:	*"And what are you looking for?"*
Client:	*"Probably at least twenty-two hundred square feet, four bedrooms."*
Salesperson:	*"Great, I know just the right home."*

Do you see the significant problem there? What exactly is the "right home?" And can we really say we have this figured out? It's bordering on arrogance to suggest having the right home at this point.

But let's see the conversation go into a different direction, using one of the most powerful questions in all of sales: *"Tell me more about that . . . "*

> *Your key phrase:*
>
> *"Tell me more about that . . . "*

Salesperson:	*"You said your home is too small. Tell me more about that."*
Client:	*"Well, the home was great when it was just my wife and I, but now our three girls are ten, twelve, and fifteen—it's cramped."*

Did that just change everything? You bet it did. But is there another level still—a deeper level of motivation? Let's see where this goes.

Salesperson:	*"What specifically isn't working? What is most frustrating about the situation?"*
Client:	*"Well, the home is eighty years old, and somehow back in those days, the builders didn't think you needed more than one bathroom. With three girls, it's kind of a problem."*

Kind of a problem? *Ya think?!* This guy is living in a home with four women and one bathroom. What do you think his life is like every morning at seven o'clock before school? And where does this guy shower—the YMCA?

Take a minute to reflect on this example. Why do you think that guy is dissatisfied with his home? Sure, the initial "why" led to stating the home is too small, but that's not the real reason. Plenty of people live in small homes and are completely satisfied. Plenty of people have only one bathroom and it works for them. So, what is it really then?

Looking closer at the situation, we can see that the deeper "why" centered around bathroom count, but again—not the real reason. Looking further into the client's situation, though, the deepest "why" ultimately led to the probable dissension and discord they experience on a daily level: the kids fighting over who gets to use the bathroom first; his wife tired and irritated that she can't get 15 minutes to put on her makeup in the morning; and he feeling frustrated that he can never get a moment to himself without someone needing to use the same space!

This guy isn't buying a bigger house or a bathroom; he's buying peace in his household.

Here's another example, courtesy of a sales representative in Houston.

Salesperson:	*"Why are you thinking about moving?"*
Client:	*"We're looking to move into the Williamson School District."*
Salesperson:	*"Tell me more about that. What is it about the school district you're in now that isn't working?"*
Client:	*"I just don't think they have the children's best interests in mind."*

Salesperson:	*"Thanks for sharing that with me. It's so hard to entrust your children to someone else and then not have the sense they're being taken care of. If you don't mind, what specifically caused you to say it's time to move away?"*
Client:	(After an awkward pause) *"Well, my son is getting bullied almost every day. I've talked to the principal and the superintendent, and they just promise to look into it. My son is starting middle school this year, and there's no way I can keep him there."*

OK, so do you think this guy wants to walk up to a salesperson and say, "Can you help me? My son is getting bullied, and I'm afraid I'm failing as a parent." Probably not. See, it takes a certain amount of trust for clients to reveal the root of their Dissatisfaction because sometimes the reasons can be embarrassingly painful or even humiliating. But that trust is established through a caring curiosity.

Until you can plumb the depths of your clients' "why," you will be stuck trying to sell with incomplete info. You will leave them to figure it out on their own.

In these case studies, we have seen a similarity of focus; all have relied on deeper curiosity and the phrase, "Tell me more about that." In fact, we see a progression with each deeper question. We move from Level 1 to Level 3:

- **Level 1:** Broad Fact
- **Level 2:** Narrow Detail
- **Level 3:** Emotional Result

It is important to understand that the highest form of selling is to meet clients' in their emotional place—that is, in Level 3. When I understand the person's Dissatisfaction on an emotional level, I can also provide an emotion-based solution.

Application Break

- Start practicing the "Tell me more about that" technique in your everyday life. Make it a point to use it tonight at dinner with your kids, or when talking on the phone to a friend, or when your spouse is downloading on the day. Then move on to the food server who waits on you, the receptionist at the dentist office who starts talking, or the taxi driver taking you to your appointment.

- "Tell me more about that" isn't only a great sales skill; it's a great life skill!

This is a long way from Sales 101; this is advanced. Think of the power of selling at this level! The chart on the following page gives you an idea of how the progression might work:

Level	Client	Salesperson
Level 1 – **Broad Fact** (*"Why are you thinking about moving?"*)	"Our home is too small."	"Great. I can show you a larger home!"
Level 2 – **Narrow Detail** (*"Tell me more about that."*)	"We have three teenage girls plus my wife and I, all sharing one bathroom."	"Great. I can show you a home with more bathrooms."
Level 3 – **Emotional Result** (*"May I ask how you are doing with that?"*)	"We are miserable. My girls fight every single morning. They just don't like each other."	"So you're not just buying bathrooms; you're buying peace in your own home."

Can you see the progression? The deeper the knowledge of the client's Dissatisfaction, especially at an emotional level, the easier it is to provide a positive emotional picture.

STUDY QUESTIONS:

1. Problem solvers use the "Three Whys Down" questioning method (ask "Why?" three times in three different ways) to get beyond a surface issue to the true root cause of a problem. Practice doing this with a homebuyer situation.

2. When you find out the underlying reason for homebuyer Dissatisfaction, what will you do with the information?

3. Think of a time when a client seemed ready to buy a house, but you just couldn't get him or her to move off the fence. What do you think the barriers were? What could you have done differently?

Chapter Six: Boldness in Questioning

I know those were tough examples and it's a lot to take in. But to be successful as salespeople, we have to deal with tough questions and understand our clients.

All this leads to definitive soul searching for the sales pro. It's time to sit down and ask two serious questions. Be honest with yourself in answering them:

- Do you have the guts to ask the deep questions?
- Are you prepared to exercise your curiosity and dig even deeper?

Remember, this isn't about you; it's about your clients.

I'm prepared to show you how to move forward in a structured and conversational way. But we have to be honest. Thorough discovery is not always comfortable. If it were, everyone would be doing it.

You see, most people opt to take the easiest route to get to where they want to go. But, as you already know, the easiest route doesn't always deliver results. If you yield to your discomfort, you will miss out on the opportunity to serve at the highest possible level.

Make a decision right now to get to know your clients more deeply and more quickly than ever before. I'll show you the technique, but you have to bring the intention. All the technique in the world is meaningless without applying it, and the application follows resolve.

So, ask yourself this: how deeply do you want to serve your clients?

From there, commit to understanding their Dissatisfaction and everything else will follow.

STUDY QUESTIONS:

1. What have you learned about yourself in this first section?

2. What is your personal area of discomfort in talking with clients?

3. How can you demonstrate that you do have the guts to ask the tough questions?

4. What actions will you take to develop your curiosity and questioning skills?

SECTION 2:

THE FORMULA FOR CHANGE

By now you have an understanding of Dissatisfaction as a motivator. You understand that not only does Dissatisfaction provide us with the desire to change our situation, but it also serves as the single most powerful force in creating urgency.

Let's go back to that ideal client in Section 1. You know, the young couple who bounced from one apartment to the other only to finally become dissatisfied with paying rent for a small, cramped space with no backyard. Or the middle-aged couple suddenly turned empty nesters in need of a smaller, more flexible home for their changing lifestyle. These client pairs are both dissatisfied with their current situations and have a desire to make a change. It's up to you as a salesperson to pinpoint the root of your clients' Dissatisfaction and turn it into a tool to help them find the right homes to fit their needs.

In this section, I'll show you how to take that Dissatisfaction and, with it, construct one of the most powerful tools in home sales. I'll also show you how clients reach a decision point, how to use a formula to evaluate every client who has ever purchased anything, and how to apply that formula to every prospect you will ever sell a home to.

You'll even see yourself in this process, because we are all motivated by Dissatisfaction every day of our lives.

In short, this formula leverages the four factors that drive the decision to buy a house. In these four areas—two action motivators and two action inhibitors—you'll see the factors that cause your clients to make one of the most important purchasing decisions most people ever make.

Let's take a look at the first of these four factors in Chapter 7.

Chapter Seven:
Motivation Factor #1:
Current Dissatisfaction

Section 1 laid out the basis behind why people move. In it, we took a look at a few of the reasons, but we can sum it all up in one word: Dissatisfaction. Here, we'll look at this action accelerator from a deeper perspective as we understand the *emotion* behind the situation.

At some point, people say to themselves, "I don't like this apartment anymore" or "Man, with six kids, this house isn't big enough." Maybe they say, "I need to entertain because of my job; I need a nicer place." Or, "This neighborhood has gone down; I don't feel my kids are safe anymore." It may be any number of things—the amenities, the changes in the clients' lives, children moving out, a job transfer, or an elderly parent moving in.

I call this condition Current Dissatisfaction, and it has nothing to do with what a client is moving *to*. Rather, the Current Dissatisfaction focuses on what the homebuyer is moving *from*.

Whatever the reason for moving, the clients sense that something in their lives isn't right, that their housing situation is no longer satisfying. By the time they arrive at your doorstep, you can be assured that every prospective client you meet is on a mission to improve the quality of his or her life. After all, if there is nothing wrong with their lives now—if everything is rainbows and unicorns—well, why make a move?

Remember from Section 1 that clients' Current Dissatisfaction is not typically found on the surface? We have to ask questions, listen, and try to understand the factors motivating our clients to buy a home. Finding out this motivation requires that deeper probing.

This concept represents a dividing line between *average* and *great* sales professionals. Most salespeople will, if only by accident, stumble on their prospect's Current Dissatisfaction. But the key to leveraging that Current Dissatisfaction is understanding it on an *emotional* level.

> "If there is Dissatisfaction with the status quo, good. If there is ferment, so much the better. If there is restlessness, I am pleased. Then let there be ideas, and hard thought, and hard work. If man feels small, let man make himself bigger."
>
> **Hubert H. Humphrey**

This is a critically important principle to grasp: people don't buy because of their Dissatisfaction; they buy because of their emotional response to their Dissatisfaction. A prospect might say, "My home is too small," but the real motivation will have to do with his or her frustration in living in a small home. That could be tied to any number of things: friction between kids; lack of privacy; annoyance during dinner preparation; even embarrassment in having people over. Notice that these real issues are all emotional, not logical.

Author and business entrepreneur Nido Qubein offers a helpful insight: "People don't buy products. They buy the solutions that the products represent."

As an example, a 30-something couple walks in and, by all appearances, are doing well financially. They pull up in a late model mini-van or SUV wearing trendy clothes and waving around the latest gadgets. If you were just a spectator looking in on the situation, you might make some assumptions about their jobs, their social status, and their spending power. But making assumptions doesn't get us any closer to the heart of the issue; it only sets us up for failure.

After a few minutes of introductions and chitchat, you ask these questions: what are you looking to spend, where do you want to live, what kind of amenities? After the usual responses about the neighborhood, kitchen is too small, living area is tiny, and so on, the truth comes out: their current kitchen has outdated countertops; they have cracked marble tile in the entryway; the carpet is *shag*. Somewhere in the middle of all this explanation, the wife blurts out, "I'm just too embarrassed to have company over, and we need to start entertaining. I would die if my coworkers or my husband's ever saw our house!"

> "People don't buy products. They buy the solutions that the products represent."
>
> **Nido Qubein**

And there it is—at the emotional level. It isn't the countertops or the tile or the carpet. Those can all be fixed with remodeling. It's the *embarrassment*. It's the Current Dissatisfaction motivating this couple to buy a newer, more stylish house.

Following are three case studies that show how the Dissatisfaction on the surface doesn't reveal the emotional factors that truly drive a decision.

Case Study #1: A man comes into a sales office and, upon questioning, shares that his home backs up to a busy street. The salesperson responds, "Tell me more about that" and the prospect replies, "The street is where the teenagers go cruising on the weekends. Then they pull over to talk, but their radios are blaring. I have no peace and I also have safety concerns." The initial response ("busy street") is far too vague to constitute an action driver. Only with deeper probing do we understand the real concerns—peace and safety.

Case Study #2: A woman tells a Realtor she wants to downsize. Many salespeople would take this in the direction of "What size home do you have?" and "What size home are you looking for?" A better Realtor says, "Tell me more about that." He discovers the woman has been hanging on to her large home for too long, that she took a huge cut in pay to keep her job and can no longer handle the payments. Her real motivation is financial peace, not square footage.

Case Study #3: A man at an open house says, "I'm tired of renting." The salesperson asks why and he responds that there's an ongoing feud with the neighbors over the volume of their stereo, that the landlord refuses to do anything about it, and that he recently had his tires slashed. "Tired of renting" is *not* a motivation to move, but Fear certainly is.

Consider the examples on the following page showing common statements of motivation and where the actual Dissatisfaction might lie:

Discovery Level One	Discovery Level Two	Discovery Level Three
Current home backs to busy street.	Lots of traffic, thus a safety concern. (How many salespeople would have assumed a noise problem?)	Third time a family cat has been lost to traffic—a highly emotional issue.
Relocating from out of state.	This relocation is optional; the family is on a discovery trip.	Husband is excited about the move; wife is heavily resistant.
Couple looking for more bedrooms.	Currently living in a three-bedroom place looking for five.	Couple is newly engaged, both with kids from previous marriages.

Application Break

- Brainstorm different ways to say, "Tell me more about that." Understanding Current Dissatisfaction is always about digging far below the surface. If you can become familiar with several different probing questions, your questioning will come off more natural and less threatening.

- Whenever you meet a prospective client this week, think about the Three Whys. Commit to digging down to this third level of understanding. When you do, you'll find that this is the level where the emotion resides.

One last thing to know about the clients Current Dissatisfaction: it doesn't happen overnight. It brews and festers until your clients can't take it anymore. Usually by that point, they've already made it into your office.

This is good news. We've heard the dreaded words, "We just started looking." Typically, our hearts sink at that statement. We feel frustrated knowing people have to go through a long process, and they are just at the start, right?

Except for one thing—it's not true. They did not, in fact, "just start looking." They've been looking for a long time, certainly as long as they've lived with significant Dissatisfaction.

The couple who walked in and told you their home is too small is an example. It's not like they woke up this very morning, got out of bed, looked around, and suddenly proclaimed, "Say, this house is too small! When did that happen? Honey, I don't know what plans we had today, but we're going house hunting instead."

No. That home has been too small for years! The Dissatisfaction has been brewing a long time. Now they can't take it anymore, and they land in your office.

> *Current Dissatisfaction brews over a long period, and it's always increasing.*

The truth is, they wanted to move yesterday. Now it's your turn to help connect them with the Future Promise waiting for them.

STUDY QUESTIONS:

1. When was the last time you bought a new home? How long were you living with your own Current Dissatisfaction before you started looking for something else?

2. What is your Current Dissatisfaction in your present home? Create a list and consider how your own Dissatisfaction escalates over time.

3. What would you do if one client admits to a Current Dissatisfaction but the spouse or partner does not?

4. With your current clients, fill out the table of Discovery Levels 1, 2, and 3. (If you can't quite do this exercise now, you'll gain insights in the coming chapters, then come back to complete it.)

Chapter Eight:
Motivation Factor #2:
Future Promise

If a compelling Current Dissatisfaction exists, there's also a compelling Future Promise, which is the second of our motivation factors. The Future Promise represents the hopes and dreams of the new home and of a new life. It also represents the solution to the emotional pain of the Current Dissatisfaction.

> *"As for the future, your task is not to foresee it, but to enable it."*
>
> **Antoine de Saint-Exupery**

Your clients' Future Promise represents the picture in their minds of what their lives could be like. It's the hope of things to come when they move forward. It could be tied to the home itself, to the yard, to the neighborhood or the schools, or to just about anything else the clients look forward to. Typically, it's a combination of all those things.

Specifically, the Future Promise is a mental construct that guides clients on their search, a fuzzy image of an undefined ideal. You've likely heard prospects say something like, "I'll know it when I see it."

Here's what I believe they're actually saying: *They'll know it when they see it!* The Future Promise is not always clear in the clients' minds, especially in the early part of the homebuying journey.

The Future Promise represents the hopes and dreams of the new home and of a new life.

Let me ask you this: What do you suspect is behind all the design shows on HGTV? Or why are there racks of magazines with photos of beautiful kitchens? Is it to sell product? Of course it is. But what's the appeal of these products? To have better countertops so they last longer? Maybe. To have more efficient water usage with shiny new faucets? That has to be considered. But honestly, these products *play on the hopes and dreams of what could be.* They appeal to the motivation of Future Promise.

But like the Current Dissatisfaction, the Future Promise isn't fully understood until we uncover it on its *emotional* terms. It isn't only about the nice kitchen or another bedroom. It's about the pleasure of life. It's about the sense of peace when the kids have their own space. Or the vast yard space that they are lacking today. Or the great room that allows for the ultimate in informal entertaining. Or the master suite that provides an escape from four active and loud children.

Typically, too many salespeople get stuck on "what are you looking for?" because they're trained that way. It's ingrained in their minds to look for the sale by meeting the obvious need. But this question should get at a more important point: "*Why* are you looking for it?" This is the deeper, emotional motivation that needs to be met.

Let's look at a few scenarios to discover the power of the Future Promise at a deeper level.

SCENARIO 1

Salesperson:	*"How many bedrooms are you looking for?"*
Client:	*"Four."*
Salesperson:	*"OK, got it. And are you looking for a one-story or two-story?"*

WRONG! This follow-up question doesn't connect at the emotional level. Let's try that again.

SCENARIO 2

Salesperson:	*"What are some of the 'must-haves' on your list?"*
Client:	*"We need to have four bedrooms."*
Salesperson:	*"OK, got it. Tell me more about that. Why four?"*
Client:	*"We have two teenagers, a boy and a girl. Because of my job, sometimes I have to make overseas calls at odd hours. Right now, I work from a home office in the corner of the master bedroom. When I have to make these calls in the early hours, it's a real problem."*

As you can see in the second scenario, this buyer isn't buying just another bedroom. He's buying both the pride of his own office space and a remedy to the inconvenience of early morning phone calls while his wife sleeps. In effect, he's buying a solution to his Current Dissatisfaction.

The top performing salesperson is wise to always consider the "why" behind the "what." Remember, every "what?" question demands a "why?" follow up. For example:

Salesperson:	*"What is most important to you in your new home?"*
Client:	*"Yard space. We'd love to have at least eight thousand square feet."*
Salesperson:	*"Tell me why eight thousand. How did you arrive at that?"*
Client:	*"We are avid swimmers and would like to put in a large pool. But we also have two dogs so we need some lawn space."*

In this example, I learned important information to help me determine which home might be right to show them, and I also learned about their lives. This allows for a deeper sense of connection.

Application Break

- If you are working with clients who have a hard time verbalizing what they are looking for ("We'll know it when we see it"), try to find the Future Promise by understanding more about the home they are in now. A good question to ask would be, *"Tell me about the home you are in right now. What do you love about, and what do you hate about it?"*

THE CURRENT DISSATISFACTION – FUTURE PROMISE CONNECTION

Before moving on to the next factor in our formula, here's one more intriguing thing to understand about Future Promise: a strong Future Promise can actually serve to boost the client's Current Dissatisfaction!

Let's suppose your best friend buys a brand new car and wants to take you out to lunch to celebrate. Of course, she will drive. You meet up somewhere and get out of your perfectly satisfactory car and into her new car. As you get in, you notice several cool things:

- That wonderful new car smell
- The push-button ignition that works while the key stays in her purse
- The back-up camera on the dashboard
- The air-conditioned seats

After lunch, your friend drops you off and you get back into your old car. Now what happens?

- You take a big whiff and ask, "What is that smell?"
- You have to fumble for your keys in your purse.
- You have to crank your head to look behind you when backing up.
- Your seat is blistering hot on this summer day.

Before you first sat in your friend's brand new car, you were perfectly happy with your own. Where are you now? Pointed in the direction of a car dealership!

This works in home sales as well. Clients might be moderately dissatisfied with their current house but not enough to make a move. Not yet, anyway. They claim they are "just looking," and to a point, they actually believe that. Imagine, however, that they walk into a home with a tricked-out master suite. Or a house with lots of storage space, a vaulted ceiling, large windows, a sitting room, a dual-sided fireplace. Or closets big enough to waltz in, a soaking tub with Jacuzzi jets, towel warmers . . . the dream bedroom.

Until now, they were fairly satisfied with their master suite. It got the job done and didn't cause any problems. Their Current Dissatisfaction was relatively low. But now they see an amazing Future Promise, and their Current Dissatisfaction skyrockets. Suddenly, their present master bedroom seems tiny, plain, and boring compared to the tricked-out suite they saw in the house they were just shown. Now they're thinking about the inadequacies of their current home and how much better life could be in a new place with more features and better amenities.

If your clients don't lead off by showing high Current Dissatisfaction, don't panic. It may be they haven't acknowledged the need at an emotional level yet, that they don't know what's available. Sometimes Current Dissatisfaction develops once your clients see what options and amenities are available as part of the Future Promise.

> *A compelling Future Promise can elevate your client's Current Dissatisfaction.*

STUDY QUESTIONS:

1. Throughout your career, you've seen a lot of homes with wonderful amenities. If you were in the market for a new home now, what would you include in your Future Promise? Make a written list.

2. Compare your Future Promise list to the Current Dissatisfaction list you made for the last chapter. What items might you add to your Current Dissatisfaction list given that you've thought about Future Promise?

3. Think about your current clients. Where are they in articulating their Current Dissatisfaction and Future Promise items? How can you help them discuss and even write down their thoughts?

Chapter Nine:
Inhibitor Factor #1: Cost

While the Current Dissatisfaction and the Future Promise work together to move clients forward, two inhibitors can hold them back. The first of these is Cost. Let's define that; it is not as simple as it might seem.

Most homebuyers associate Cost with the total price tag on a home, the bottom-line sales price as stated on the purchase agreement. We all know, of course, that one cannot consider price alone. So Cost is better defined as representing every price the client will have to pay, even the non-financial ones.

"There are risks and costs to action. But they are far less than the long range risks of comfortable inaction."

John F. Kennedy

Here are examples of Cost, both monetary and non-monetary:

- **Selling Price** – Think of its price as a value gauge on the home. The selling price is not in and of itself a financial burden unless the client is paying cash. But the price does represent a sense of comparative worth as well as being an indicator of ability to pay and, as an extension, ability to qualify for loans.

- **Payment** – The price is but a value gauge; the payment is where the rubber meets the road. Mortgage payments—the part that hurts every single month. Is this "new pain" really worth it? "What types of sacrifices will I have to make when I purchase this home? Can I still live the lifestyle I desire? Will we have to suffer in terms of quality of vacations or how often we eat out?"

- **Time** – Buying a home and moving takes time. Your client has to take time from work or use weekends to look, get qualified, pack, unpack, and so on. Purchasing a home is not a simple endeavor; the process eats up a significant amount of time for any homebuyer.

- **Hassle** – Imagine if I asked you to take two days off for a project, and on day one instructed you to pack up your garage and let the boxes sit where they were. Then on day two, you'd unpack the boxes and put everything back. How would you feel about that? Horrified, probably! But your client has to think in terms of the whole house: all of the garage, all of the kitchen, all of the knick-knacks collected over the years, all of the yard toys—ugh! Buying a home is a gigantic hassle, and inconvenience is a huge Cost.

- **Down payment** – Paying 20% down on a $300,000 home is $60,000. I don't know how else to look at it except saying that's a lot of money. Does your client really want to part with something that probably took years to acquire? Will the return be worthwhile? What are the other investment options for that cash? Will it drain the reserves?

- **New Costs** – Is there a homeowners' association with monthly fees? Will the taxes be higher in the new home versus the old home? Will the clients have to put their kids in a new school or even a private school? Will the energy bills cost more? Is there garbage service and will it have an out-of-pocket cost? And then there's always this thought: "What else am I missing?"

- **Compromise** – Every dollar spent is a dollar that's unavailable for something else. So, when clients buy a home, they are committing to that mortgage payment, often at the expense of other things they'd like to have and do (e.g., cars, vacations, private school, etc.).

> *The salesperson who thinks that Cost only equals sales price is in for a difficult awakening!*

Application Break

- Think of a client you recently sold a home to. What were the most significant aspects of Cost, apart from the price? Now brainstorm the questions (in your own words) that might help you understand your client's Cost concerns.

HOW DEALS DESTROY VALUE PERCEPTIONS

Undoubtedly, Cost is a significant inhibitor. In fact, the Cost factor scares a great many *salespeople*. That's one reason why many sales professionals take a proactive (though faulty) approach by talking about discounts and deals right off the bat. (Big mistake, by the way.)

Sellers who lead with their discount or their willingness to deal do more than just lower their profit. They cause a devaluing of the product. And not just a financial devaluing, either. Clients literally think less of what they're actually buying.

Consider the Macy's department store approach. When is Macy's not having a sale? And on top of the sale, how about its "Preferred Customer Coupon"? And the mysterious 50%-off rack in the corner, the one with the rider that says, "Today only—take an additional 25% off"? And what's with the "White Flower Day" anyway? That's just making up an excuse to discount.

At Macy's, while customers feel good about the discounted price, they also discount the quality of the merchandise. In their own minds, they think items that are easily obtained are lightly esteemed. "Yes, I got a good deal, but I'm not all that in love with the merchandise." Are you with me on this point?

Do this mental exercise. Do you have an item of clothing right now that you've owned for 30 days or more and still have the price tags attached? If you're like most people, the answer is "yes." Next question: did you get it on sale? Again, the majority would say they did. Now think of an item of apparel—perhaps something you're wearing right now—that you paid full price for. How soon after you purchased it did you wear it? Right away, I bet.

Similarly, when a salesperson brings up discounts and encourages offers right off the bat, this devalues the perception of the home in the homebuyers' eyes. If this strategy is being encouraged, then the clients question if the house was overpriced to begin with, that this discount strategy was already accounted for. So then, they suspect, the house isn't worth what's being asked. The perceived value has already dropped and may serve to steer them away from making an offer.

Therefore, as a salesperson, you may actually be doing your clients a huge disservice talking about discounts. You may, in all reality, be steering them *away* from the house of their dreams—their Future Promise!

STUDY QUESTIONS:

1. How does a discounted price on a house make potential clients feel about the value of the home?

2. We've articulated some of the Costs of buying a new home. What are some of the existing and potentially increasing Costs of staying in the current home? How would you use this information to help clients who are struggling with the perceived Cost of the new home based on its listed price?

3. If the Cost of "hassle" weighs heavily with a client, what can you do to help overcome that hurdle?

4. "Time is money." How does working through a systematic process to getting homebuyers off the fence and into a new home quickly save them money?

Chapter Ten:
Inhibitor Factor #2: Fear

The final factor is related to Cost but is best approached from the emotional perspective. Though sometimes overlooked, the clients' level of Fear is so important, it cannot be ignored. Even clients with a high Current Dissatisfaction who have seen an incredible Future Promise can have an overwhelming and even debilitating level of Fear.

Years ago, a client called me and said he desperately needed to sell his home and get it closed—*in the next 72 hours.* He was going through a messy divorce and he needed this asset off the books in a hurry. That meant an all-cash deal at a deep discount. While the home's condition was a little rough, it had an amazing location and an incredible price.

> *"I learned that courage was not the absence of fear, but the triumph over it. The brave man is not he who does not feel afraid, but he who conquers that fear."*
>
> **Nelson Mandela**

I wasn't in a position to buy it at the time, but I figured I could get a fellow Realtor to bite. First, however, I offered it to my in-laws. I called the folks and rushed them over to show the home. I was so excited I couldn't stand it—a rare deal that come along once in a blue moon.

My mother-in-law walked through the home and got an immediate negative impression: old carpet infested with cat fleas. My father-in-law noted the dry rot around the tub in the bathroom. I watched them view the home with disgust on their faces. I couldn't believe it; this was a rare opportunity and they were consumed with cosmetic issues!

In the end, they passed on the home. I sold it "all cash" later that afternoon to a Realtor. An interesting side note: the home sold four years later for four times what the Realtor paid, a 400% value increase.

Even clients with a high Current Dissatisfaction and who have seen an incredible Future Promise can experience an overwhelming and even debilitating level of Fear.

To this day, my in-laws still regret their shortsightedness. For the longest time, I thought they were simply foolish. But over time, I came to understand that their response wasn't unlike most people making a highly emotional decision. The Fear is absolutely gripping.

THE SALES "COUNSELOR"

An important function of a real estate salesperson is to understand the homebuyers' Fear, cope with it, and help them overcome it. This is where the term "sales counselor" comes into play. Whether we like it or not, we play the role of junior psychologist from time to time.

Yet too many salespeople are afraid to plumb the depths of their clients' Fears. They worry that if clients talk about Fear, it will elevate the concern and possibly spoil the sale. I disagree, and I advocate taking an entirely different approach.

As a salesperson, if I don't know what's bothering my clients, it doesn't lessen their Fears. In fact, it may serve to *promote* those Fears. They can feel they're all alone in this endeavor, that they're being misunderstood or even misinformed. This will heighten their emotions and especially their Fear. And that's not good. This type of misunderstanding leads clients to distrust salespeople and believe all salespeople are just out to make that quick sale and disappear.

It pays to know what your clients' deepest Fears are.

Put yourself in their shoes for a moment, if you will. A homebuyer's extensive Fears can lead to a number of troubling questions:

- Do I really want to move in the first place? Am I *really* that unhappy with it? (Is my Current Dissatisfaction high enough?)
- Is this the right home? Will this meet my needs? (Do I see enough Future Promise?)
- Is this the right time to move, or should I wait?
- What will happen in the economy? In my job?
- What will my kids think? My neighbors? My parents?
- Are interest rates likely to go lower if I wait? Higher?
- What if I buy and then the price goes down?
- Are these the right schools?
- How long will the commute be?
- How much money will I have to spend after I move in?
- Will I regret this move?

Those Fears, and many more, are real and ever-present. As a salesperson, you need to address them or, at the very least, acknowledge them. If Fears aren't handled properly, they can be the cause for buyers' remorse. I believe the key to handling these Fears is openness and honesty. Get your clients to talk through their Fears and encourage them to hold nothing back.

Application Break

- If you truly want to understand your clients' Fears, then provide an atmosphere of safety in which they feel free to share. Be open and honest with your intentions, explaining that you have their best interests in mind. *"I can help you so much more if I know what's holding you back. Tell me what concerns you about any part of this process."*

THE DOWNSIDE OF FEAR

In 2001, I seriously considered purchasing stock in Apple Computers. Like all other tech stocks, it had been hammered in the dotcom bust. But I was intrigued by this new device I had purchased: an iPod. Yes, I still have a first generation iPod. It weighs about 12 pounds and holds maybe 50 songs, but it will be a collector's item for sure!

Anyway, I didn't buy the stock. Why? Fear. I was reading the reports about the death of the tech sector, as if all things technological were gone from the planet forever (sounds dumb even to write that today). I listened to fearful media reports and couldn't pull the trigger. How do you suppose that decision worked out for me?

➢ Apple Stock in September 2001: $7.75 per share

➢ Apple Stock at the time of this writing: $695.36 per share

By not making an investment of 100 shares for $775 in 2001, I missed out on $68,761 in profit today. And why? In one word: Fear.

STUDY QUESTIONS:

1. Do you have your own "Apple stock" story of an instance when you were Fearful of taking action and today recognize that your "do nothing" action was a poor decision? How can you develop that into a personal story to share with your clients?

2. President Franklin Delano Roosevelt once said, "The only thing we have to Fear is Fear itself." He was speaking of the nameless, unreasoning, unjustified terror that puts us in a state of paralysis when we need to be moving forward. How does talking with your clients about their homebuying Fears help put their Fears into a better perspective so they can be addressed and managed?

3. The list of Fears that your clients might name (see above) includes several you can address with data and projections. How would you find this information, keep it current, and use it in a fact-based, unbiased format you can share with clients as you discuss these issues?

Chapter Eleven:
The Buying Formula

So far, we've discovered the four factors that influence a homebuying decision. They are:

- Motivation Factor #1: Current Dissatisfaction
- Motivation Factor #2: Future Promise
- Inhibitor Factor #1: Cost
- Inhibitor Factor #2: Fear

Now let's see how these factors work together.

Several years ago, I developed a formula I have since taught to thousands of sales professionals around the world. The formula has been proven over and over again, not only in my own experience, but in the experience of the sales

> *"Decide that you want it more than you are afraid of it."*
>
> **Bill Cosby**

professionals who have used it. You'll see it in every transaction you've ever had, and you can apply it to every future sale.

People buy when…

Current Dissatisfaction x Future Promise > Cost + Fear

I will explain this in more detail, but for now, look closely and see how the formula works in your own experience. Recall someone who purchased from you recently. Or think of someone you have been working with who hasn't yet closed the deal. How do the categories apply?

> *If the clients' motivators do not carry more clout than their inhibitors, nothing happens.*

Let me break this down for you.

Like any math problem, all of the factors are variables. They can all be weighted or given varying importance. This formula takes everything into account, motivators and inhibitors alike. In effect, it puts them on a scale. But here's the bottom line of this formula: if the clients' *motivators* do not carry more clout than their *inhibitors*, nothing happens.

Let's suppose prospective homebuyers come to you with the following scenario:

In 2006, they bought a home at the height of the market. However, they bought in a less-desirable area because that's all they could afford at the time. Since then, the neighborhood has been in decline, and they're concerned with the safety of their children.

They've done some preliminary home search and have decided they want to purchase a home across town. To top it off, they've found one they love—a great location in the right school district with all the amenities they want.

However, its price exceeds what they want to spend. Not only that, but they are upside down on their current home and by leaving now would have to take a huge loss. In the high-tech industry, they're concerned about the broad economy and the security of their jobs.

As a salesperson, here are some questions to ask yourself about this situation:

- How high is their Current Dissatisfaction? Pretty high, right?
- How high is their Future Promise? Also very high.
- Their Cost (as defined earlier in the chapter)? WAY up there.
- How about their Fear? Sounds substantial.

For this client, *all* the factors are high. If they are to purchase, the variables need to be adjusted so the motivators outweigh the inhibitors.

As a salesperson, here are your options:

- Raise the Current Dissatisfaction
- Raise the Future Promise
- Lower the Cost
- Lower the Fear

So let me ask you, what would you do? Think about it. Right now, the clients are stagnant and not moving forward, somewhat paralyzed by their Fears. This means the scale is either equally balanced among all the factors or weighted toward the inhibitors.

> *Right now, the clients are stagnant and not moving forward, somewhat paralyzed by their Fears. Something needs to change.*

Something needs to change.

Hold that thought for a bit, and we'll get back to it. First, let's take a close look at the Buying Formula.

OBSERVATIONS ON THE BUYING FORMULA

There are some things you need to know about the formula to fully get your hands around this powerful tool. Remember, people buy when:

Current Dissatisfaction x Future Promise > Cost + Fear

1.   The formula is sequential; it's meant to be understood from left to right. Too many salespeople start with the Cost side of the formula, which is a devastating mistake. If you want to have the best chance of getting them to make a decision, learn and highlight the Current Dissatisfaction first.

2.   The left side of the formula is a multiplication function. What happens if either variable is a zero? We have a name for that kind of prospect: non-buyer. If the Current Dissatisfaction is a zero, nothing else matters—the formula will be forever out of balance.

3.   A tie goes to the inhibitor. The only way to get your client to take action is to make certain the formula favors the left side.

4.   If both the Current Dissatisfaction and the Future Promise are enormous, how much work is needed on the Cost + Fear? Answer: very, very little. That's why we start with the left-side variables.

5. The variables in the formula change over time, sometimes for the good and sometimes for the bad. At the time the client purchases, the formula is weighted in the right direction. When remorse sets in and a homebuyer cancels, it's because the Cost + Fear weighting grew.

Now go back to the case study of the home purchased in 2006. Based on the principles you just learned, how would you go about solving the problem?

To start, you'd highlight the Current Dissatisfaction. In this case, the Current Dissatisfaction likely lies with the children's safety. Based on this assumption, two questions come to my mind. First, "Do you see the situation getting better or worse over time?" Second, "Are you concerned about the safety of your children if the neighborhood continues to deteriorate?"

The idea here is to point them in the direction of inevitability. They *have* to move; it's only a matter of timing. The longer they wait, the worse it will get and could one day involve a tragic incident. Or they may lose even more money due to their declining house value.

With the Current Dissatisfaction at a high level, it's time to cement the Future Promise. Your job is to confirm that the home has everything the clients are looking for—in location, in amenities, and in Future Promise. We can cement that with an instruction or comment like this:

> *With the Current Dissatisfaction at a high level, it's time to cement the Future Promise.*

"Prices rise and fall together across all markets. If you wait for the price of your home to go up, the price on the home you are looking for will also rise. It's best to base your decision on living in the right home and in the right neighborhood."

Or,

"The price of your home has fallen, but that's a short-term consideration. You don't want to cloud your long-term decisions with short-term factors. In the long term, what will be the wiser decision: staying there or moving here?" (I already know the answer to that since the Current Dissatisfaction is maxed out!)

Only when we have determined that the Current Dissatisfaction and Future Promise are both at a high level can we work on the Cost + Fear side of the formula. Had we started with Cost + Fear, we certainly would have had our hands full.

Application Break

- Recall the last home you purchased. *Why* did you move? Was it out of Current Dissatisfaction? Future Promise? Did these outweigh Fear + Cost? Answer the question according to the formula and see if you can't find a direct application.

- Now think about the last three homes you have sold. How did the formula apply to those three clients? Go through and fill in the blank for each one. Remember the formula:

Current Dissatisfaction x Future Promise > Cost + Fear

> - Most important, think of three clients you're working with today. Where are they stuck? Are they stuck in Fear? Why have they not purchased yet? Is it because of Cost? The answer is in the formula, and when you adjust the variables, you will free up the person for further actions.

JEFF SHORE: A PERSONAL CASE STUDY

Let me share a little about my situation at the time of this writing so that you can see how the formula applies.

My wife and I have been in our home for 14 years. We moved in when our son, our oldest, was starting high school. The younger of his two sisters was in the fourth grade at the time. Now our three children are out of college and two of them are married. We live in a home that's too large for just two people, we have five acres that need to be maintained, we have a pool we do not use, and have no reason to be near the school our children attended.

That is our Current Dissatisfaction; let's look at our Future Promise.

We are looking for something that matches our lifestyle today. That means something closer to the center of town with significantly less land but still a lot of privacy. We want a home in a wooded setting that has all we need for our lifestyle: home office, drop-dead gorgeous kitchen, painting room for my wife, space for guests, bonus room for the ping-pong table, and a set-up that's dog friendly.

We do have Cost concerns since we're moving to a more expensive area and will be paying more for our home. Our taxes will also increase; so might our utility bills. Our current home has been completely remodeled, so we might have to invest in the new place to upgrade it too, to the way we want it.

Finally, we have Fear. Is this the right time to make this move? What's happening in the market? Can we sell our home for enough? Do we sell first and then purchase? Do we hold on to our current home and risk carrying two payments? What if a flood of foreclosures hit the market—will that affect home values?

I'll circle back to these four factors later in the book. For now, let's look at our actual shopping journey.

It really started *years* ago. As soon as our oldest went away to college, our home got larger and grew larger still as each child moved out. It's safe to say we've been thinking about this for years but our Dissatisfaction factor five years ago was too low to initiate action. On a 1 to 10 Dissatisfaction scale, we were probably at a 2.

When our youngest graduated from college and promptly moved to Seattle to take a job with Amazon, our Dissatisfaction escalated. We started modestly snooping around. Like most buyers, that meant spending time on-line getting a sense of what's out there. I would suggest, however, that our Current Dissatisfaction at the time was no higher than a 5—not enough to make a move.

Then something interesting happened. We started to look at homes and see the Future Promise they held. We discovered an amazing phenomenon, something I mentioned in Chapter Eight. When our Future Promise went up, our Current Dissatisfaction went up with it. We saw what could be, and it escalated our desire to move from where we are. Our Current Dissatisfaction rose to the 7 to 8 level.

Alas, the Cost + Fear is still high, especially since we haven't seen a lot of activity on our current home. Do we take the risk of buying without selling?

As of the time of this writing, I'd say that we are dead even. Our formula currently looks like this:

Current Dissatisfaction x Future Promise = Cost + Fear

Is that enough to move? No! Remember, in order to move, the motivators must *exceed* the inhibitors.

I don't know about you, but this tool excites me! Understanding and applying the formula gives me a new way to look at my clients. I gain insight as to how they think, how they make decisions, and what the roadblocks to buying might be. I can then move them out of Fear + Cost and into Current Dissatisfaction x Future Promise. How cool is that?

PUTTING THE FORMULA TO WORK

Even with this tremendous tool at your disposal, there's one more piece of the sales puzzle to consider—the structure or the "how to"—and that's where we're going next.

Coming up, I'll show you a sales structure that complements the formula. It's simple, intuitive, conversational, and in no way manipulative. One of the surest ways to kill any future sales from clients is to have them walk away feeling tricked. This destroys trust and in our profession, trust is paramount. After all, we're dealing with peoples' homes, the place where they need to feel absolutely secure and satisfied.

> *Understanding and applying the formula gives me a new way to look at my clients. I gain insight as to how they think, how they make decisions, and what the roadblocks to buying might be.*

As promised in an earlier chapter, when you know your clients well enough, they will literally show you how to sell them a home. The sales path will lay itself out right out in front of you. Your job will then be to guide them down that path.

Ready to get started?

STUDY QUESTIONS:

1. If you know your prospects have zero Current Dissatisfaction, how likely are they to really be in the market for a home?

2. How does the buying formula help explain the conflicting thoughts homebuyers struggle with as they work through the decision process?

3. Where have you focused your efforts in the past (which of the four factors)? Where do you expect to focus in the future?

4. What will you do when your clients are stuck in the situation of the left side of the formula equaling the right side?

SECTION 3:

THE 4:2 SALES FORMULA

Now, you have a good understanding of the four factors motivating your clients to make important purchasing decisions, including buying a home. People purchase when:

Current Dissatisfaction x Future Promise > Cost + Fear

So, the next big question is, how do we get the information we need about these four factors? How do we determine the varying levels of the different factors in the formula? And how do we do it with every single client?

As I mentioned before, your client won't just waltz into your office and lay down his or her hopes and Fears just like that. No, that would be too easy. Besides, part of your job as a salesperson is to use your detective skills to sniff out deeper emotional reasons behind their impetus to buy.

So, do I just hand you a set of questions with instructions to memorize them verbatim?

Well, not exactly. Let's take a look at what works.

Chapter Twelve:
Standardized Scripting vs.
Strategic Structure

Think back to the first sales you ever made. Chances are, you used at least parts of a standardized script you'd learned in training. And although the script probably wasn't that exciting by the time you practiced it for the 27th time, it worked. Ask veteran salespeople and they'll likely tell you the best way to learn to sell is by using a structured questioning pattern, like a script. And a script is essentially that, a structured questioning pattern.

Here's the problem: too many salespeople get stuck as they struggle to remember the lines of the script. They stammer and strain to come up with the exact wording, especially in the stressful heat of the moment.

> *"I think a playwright realizes after he finishes working on the script that this is only the beginning. What will happen when it moves into three dimensions?"*
>
> **Don DeLillo**

And, yet, learning a strategically structured sales pattern is vital to the success of any sales presentation. In fact, just learning it isn't enough. It must be drilled so deeply into the subconscious that you don't have to think about it. With the process deeply ingrained, you're freed to connect with your clients on an emotionally deeper level. Once you have it down, there's no longer a need for the script. You know the pattern and can adapt it to your client. In fact, that structure must be so deeply ingrained into your mind that you don't even have to think about it—you've become unconsciously competent.

Here's an interesting paradox; it might sound strange, but let me put this out there: sales professionals must master their presentations so well that they become liberated from thinking about their presentations.

Wait! Say that again?

> *Sales professionals must master their presentations so well that they are liberated from thinking about the presentation; they are freed up to focus on the client!*

OK, let's think this through.

My son Kevin was quite the actor all through school, culminating in playing every actor's dream role his senior year in college: Willy Loman in *Death of a Salesman*. One thing about Kevin—he always had his lines down well before he was required to. He memorized as quickly as he could. As soon as he got the script, he was committing every line to his subconscious.

I asked Kevin why he was dedicated to memorizing the lines so early. His response made perfect sense and provides great insight for salespeople. To make the transition, simply insert "selling" whenever you see "acting."

In Kevin's words:

"Acting is not simply the sharing of lines. It is all about the connection with the person in front of you. When I am acting, it is critical that I not be thinking about my lines. To do so would cost me—I would not be able to deeply connect with my partner. Great acting is when the lines are down so solidly that you don't have to think about the lines. Instead, you think about the nuances of the interaction with the person standing in front of you."

So, as you can see, it's the same thing with a salesperson. Like an actor, we have to "learn our lines." If we fail to do a good job at learning them, we might get stuck just when the action gets going. But those who have learned the script inside and out can take liberties, do a little improvising, and still stay right on track with the script. We haven't sacrificed our structured sales pattern.

That's what it truly means to have your presentation down solid. It is so ingrained in your memory that you don't even have to think about it. Instead, you're free to think about what's most important... your client!

You become free to respond to what you learn, to probe deeper, to understand the emotion behind the statement. You go with the flow of your clients, making a connection, and fully listening to what they have to say.

If only all salespeople handled their clients like this, right? Instead, too many get stuck thinking about their next lines or aiming to impart a bit of trivial wisdom on their clients. When they do this, they're not really paying attention to the deeper messages the clients need them to hear. This eventually drives clients away.

When I first read *The Seven Habits of Highly Successful People,* I came across this gem of an idea from the late Stephen Covey in discussing Habit Five: "Seek First to Understand, Then to Be Understood." Covey said, "Most people do not listen with the intent to understand; they listen with the intent to respond."

Ouch. I felt like I'd been kicked in the gut on that one. It cut me to the core.

Surely you know the feeling of halfway listening to a prospect and the whole time thinking, "When you shut up, I have something powerful to say." But when you do this, you're not *really* listening with the intent to deeply understand.

It's this kind of thinking that puts us in a position of not focusing on the client at all. Instead, we're more focused on ourselves and whether we've got our presentation down or not.

However, when you have your presentation down solid, you are now free to not think about it at all. You have the freedom to understand your clients on dramatically deep levels.

THE KEY TO EFFECTIVE SKILL DEVELOPMENT

How does one reach this level of proficiency? Your initial response was probably to say, "Practice!" And you'd be partially right. There is no question; practice is critical to success in any endeavor. But it's not enough.

Too many sales professionals practice only as long as they are required to do so. They practice in a training session or, if they are ambitious, in the car from time to time. Top professionals know it takes more than just practicing once or twice. Rather, it's good to practice until you can barely stand the sound of your own voice.

In short, it's not just about practicing; it's about *repetition.* As the saying goes, "Amateurs practice until they get it right. Professionals practice until they can't get it wrong." Truer words were never spoken. Great performances—in music, in theater, in athletics, *and* in sales— are based on endless repetition.

Application Break

- Try this self-training exercise: think of one technique, however small, that you might be able to perfect through repetition. Perhaps it's how you explain a contract clause or "NextGen" housing. Or perhaps it's simply how you exchange names when someone first walks into your open house.

- Practice that technique ten times out loud, working on the specific tone and phrasing. Then record on your smart phone and listen back. Adjust the presentation, practice out loud five more times, then record it again.

- Practice sounds monotonous and, like playing the scales on the piano, it is. But the repetition cements proper technique into your brain. Start with something small and really nail it. You'll see the effect it can have the next time you use that technique.

The chapters that follow lay out the opportunity to revolutionize the first five minutes of your sales presentation. Most important, you'll learn more critical information about your clients in the first five minutes than most people learn in the entire presentation.

But the execution of the principles is up to you. Sure, I'll show you how to practice repeatedly, but it will only be through your personal fortitude that you can take your presentation from good to great.

STUDY QUESTIONS:

1. When was the last time you actually practiced something so you knew it cold? (That bit of Shakespeare you had to memorize in high school English?)

> *Amateurs practice until they get it right. Professionals practice until they can't get it wrong.*

2. Have you read Stephen Covey's book, *The Seven Habits of Highly Effective People?* If not, at least give it a skim. How can you apply some of his suggestions to improve the effectiveness of your listening skills, especially from Habit Five?

3. How well do you really listen? If you're the kind of person who likes to prepare a response while "listening" or jump in before people finish their thoughts, how will you break these bad habits?

Chapter Thirteen:
Why vs. What

In the next chapter, I will share with you The 4:2 Formula or pattern that will provide the structure you need to understand your clients and, based on that understanding, how you can accomplish the elusive sales nirvana called "mutual purpose."

The 4:2 Formula relies heavily on "why" questions vs. "what" questions.

> *"Always the beautiful answer who asks a more beautiful question."*
>
> **e.e. cummings**

This is important because "why" questions help your clients talk about the real motivations that have them looking for a home and the deeper reasons behind the "what" factors. Once you know those reasons, it's fairly simple to figure out the "what" that will be the solution to their dilemma. Chapter 5 spoke in depth about the difference between "what" and "why"; however, let's get to an even deeper level than that.

Here's the problem I see in training sessions all the time: it's quite possible that you are unconsciously competent at the *wrong things*. You might be thinking, "Hold on there, big guy—I've got my structured sales pattern down pat; I've got this figured out. I know my sales structure." Challenge yourself on that.

The fact is, the overwhelming percentage of salespeople are stuck on "what" questions. They ask these "what" questions almost automatically, firing them off at their clients like a shotgun:

> *You need to ask yourself: "Am I a 'why' salesperson or a 'what' salesperson?"*

- *"What are you looking for in a home?"*
- *"What kind of neighborhood/school district are you looking for?"*
- *"What's the most important feature in a home to you?"*

Even in training sessions, in situations when I explicitly instruct them to ask "why" instead of "what" questions, they can't help it—a "what" question comes out.

Stop it already!

There are many ways to connect with clients and increase your sales. But, if you can't identify the "why," how will you ever be able to determine the "what" that becomes your solution?

Such is the power of habits, which is exactly why we're talking about this. I know old habits die hard, but we need to have this conversation. You won't be able to master the 4:2 pattern with "what"-based questions, an archaic and outdated method. So, my challenge is to begin harnessing the power of "why" so you might see how your sales approach changes for the better.

Application Break

- To practice your "why" questions, start with something very, very common like a bedroom count. Most salespeople learn the bedroom count early on in the process; at times it's the first piece of information we receive about a new client. A minority of salespeople dig deeper to find the "why" behind the "what."

- Build this into your discovery habit. As soon as you ascertain the bedroom count (either because you asked or they offered), immediately ask the reasons behind the bedroom count. "Okay – three bedrooms? Obviously a master. How will the other two be used?"

- You could find that the "why" response might lead you to understand that "three bedrooms" might not be necessary at all! (More about that later in the book.)

In the implementation section, I'll offer specific drills to break those old habits and replace them with new healthier sales behaviors.

For now, just be aware. When you catch yourself asking "what" questions, stop and think them through. Make a conscious effort to ask "why" questions with each and every client you work with. Have your coworkers, spouse, or a good friend listen to your presentation and point this out. A conscious effort to change your approach is the only way to affect long-term change.

Just be aware—that's only half the battle.

STUDY QUESTIONS:

1. If you can, record yourself giving your sales presentation or role modeling a client interaction with a friend or family member. Listen to the recording and jot down the questions you asked. How many were "what" and how many were "why" questions?

2. How would you convert your most common "what" questions to "why" questions?

3. Why are "why" questions so powerful?

Chapter Fourteen:
The 4:2 Formula

Let's start out by taking a look at The 4:2 Formula from a bird's-eye view and drill down as we go along, shall we?

The 4:2 Formula is all about getting to know the clients on a deep level and allowing the sale to roll out in front of you. In many ways, this technique is a lot like most martial arts—not aggressive but more of a reactive approach. You're using the clients' energy, the information they are giving you, to help them narrow their focus in an extremely cooperative approach.

> *"If you put water into a cup, it becomes the cup. You put water into a bottle; it becomes the bottle. You put it into a teapot; it becomes the teapot. Water can flow, or it can crash. Be water, my friend..."*
>
> **Bruce Lee**

This is not to suggest that, in using this technique, you'll find your demonstration skills to be unimportant (they are!), or that you don't have to close the sale (you do!); it's just not the focus of this book.

That said, if you get The 4:2 Formula right, you will find that showing your client the right home is infinitely easier. You'll find the close is completely conversational and entirely logical to both parties. The 4:2 Formula is a tool that serves you throughout the sales process.

OK, so let's have a look at the entire process from the top down:

The 4:2 Formula = 4 Discovery Categories + 2 Summary Questions

The 4 Discovery Categories:

✓ Trust Building
✓ Motivation Questions
✓ Current Dissatisfaction Questions
✓ Future Promise Questions

The 2 Summary Questions:

✓ The Summary Dissatisfaction Question
✓ The Summary Solution Question

The 4:2 Formula					
4 Discovery Categories				2 Summary Questions	
1. Trust Building	2. Motivation Questions	3. Current Dissatisfaction Questions	4. Future Promise Questions	1. Summary Dissatisfaction Question	2. Summary Solution Question

As we continue, you'll understand that the purpose of The 4:2 Formula is to use the "4"—the initial categories of questions—to get to the "2"—the underlying cause and solution. You see, the "2" is where the money is. This is where you establish a shared mission and where you offer clients a viable solution. It's a beautiful thing.

When you have completed The 4:2 Formula, you will have established mutual purpose, which is a shared vision regarding where you are and where you're going. You'll be on the same page with your clients and have proven you have their best interests in mind.

Too many clients see the sales presentation as an "us vs. them" endeavor. Alas, many salespeople see it the same way. They take a *Glengarry Glen Ross* manipulative mindset into the meeting with a new client. That is, they believe (or have been trained) that sales is about trickery and manipulation.

I'll assume that doesn't represent your wishes. Frankly, if it did, you would have bailed out on this book by now! I'm here to talk to those who see sales as a valuable service to their clients, and those who see salespeople as contributing to the societal good. I suggest we do this most effectively when we seek to join our clients in their quest to improve their own lives.

Having a mutual purpose with your client catapults you to a different plane of operation within the sales process. Mutual purpose is about being on the same page with clients helping them achieve their goals. It's also about agreeing with them on how their lives need to improve and how you can help. Having a mutual purpose makes the rest of the conversation silky smooth because you're now both working toward the same goal.

> *Too many clients see the sales presentation as an "us vs. them" endeavor.*

With mutual purpose, you will move beyond salesperson and into the much-coveted role of Trusted Advisor.

So are you ready to establish mutual purpose with your clients? Well then, let's do it!

STUDY QUESTIONS:

1. Why is achieving a mutual purpose valuable?

2. Think back on your most recent half-dozen clients. How many of those interactions could be characterized as having mutual purpose?

3. Pick one or two of these that weren't successful. What do you know about the client that would have helped you become a Trusted Advisor?

Chapter Fifteen:
Discovery Category #1:
Trust Building

The first step in the sales structure is to establish a deep sense of Trust as a foundation for the buyer-seller relationship. That might sound like I'm channeling Captain Obvious here, but I'm going to put some new spins on the idea.

> *"To be trusted is a greater compliment than being loved."*
>
> **George MacDonald**

Let's talk about what we're trying to do—and what we're *not* trying to do.

From time to time, I hear a salesperson (usually a long-time veteran) say something like this: "I don't care if they like me; I just want them to buy from me!"

Let me ask you this: is it possible to sell a home to someone who doesn't like you? Yes, it's possible, *but it's really, really hard!*

Would you buy something from someone you didn't like? Surely you have, but you probably don't remember that person and if you do, that memory isn't positive.

Now think about a time you purchased something from someone you
really liked. You probably remember
that person fairly well; you might even
still have his or her business card hang-

> *People like to do business with people who are likable.*

ing on your fridge. You probably recall liking the person because he
or she seemed genuinely interested in you and your best interests.
Chances are you wouldn't hesitate to refer that person to your friends
and family.

This gives us an understanding as to why likability is a critically
important variable in the study of influence theory. In fact, it's one of
the six principles highlighted by Robert Cialdini in his landmark book
Influence: The Psychology of Persuasion (an absolute must-read for every salesperson).

> *"Few people would be surprised to learn that, as a rule, we most
> prefer to say yes to the requests of someone we know and like. What
> might be startling to note, however, is that this simple rule is used
> in hundreds of ways by total strangers to get us to comply with their
> requests." (Cialdini, Influence, page 167)*

Being likable has proven scientific benefits for a salesperson. But
can the pursuit of likability go too far? Of course it can. Sometimes too
much of a good thing is, well, just too much. I've seen many a salesperson take this to a level that actually cripples the sales process. Maybe
you've experienced this yourself. Or perhaps you've seen another salesperson in your office attempting the overly friendly approach, only to
get burned in the end.

They try to become fast friends and proceed to lose their objectiv-
ity. They also worry about offending the clients, even becoming afraid

to voice their opinion or object to something that's not in their clients' best interest.

For example, say clients are convinced they can get away with purchasing a home outside of their means. Because the salesperson is afraid of offending them by pointing out otherwise, he or she goes along with the purchase. After viewing one over-budget home after another, the clients deem the salesperson incompetent and move on. If only the salesperson had spoken up earlier. Ultimately, the buyer-seller relationships are rendered non-functional.

Remember, it's your responsibility as a Trusted Advisor to educate your clients about the best solutions for them. You're not there primarily to make a new friend—although it's great when it does happen. You're there to make a sale. Don't forget that!

Let me offer you this mindset; it's a concept with which I've gotten a lot of traction with salespeople.

The goal is not to develop your new BFF (remember, you're a Trusted Advisor). Nor is it to find someone to vacation with (you've got plenty of those). In fact, those things involve too much pressure, too much commitment from both parties. Therefore, the goal of your relationship needs to be simpler than that.

Stop for a moment and ask yourself this question:

"Am I coffee-worthy? Five minutes into this conversation would this prospect want to have a cup of coffee with me?"

Consider the question from your own perspective. What are characteristics of a person *you* would want to have a cup of coffee with? Go ahead, list them on paper. What kinds of qualities do you come up with?

- Friendly
- Interested in me

- Engaged and engaging

- Good listener

- Good-natured

- Expressive body language

- Excellent eye contact

- Confident

Aren't those what you'd look for when you meet someone for the first time? I know I would.

Now, imagine you were meeting a salesperson who shared exactly those qualities. Would you be OK with the thought of having coffee with him or her?

The coffee-worthy test gives us a different standard for the rapport-building process. It's about purpose and intentionality more than about technique and scripts. In fact, I am purposely omitting ideas on how to chitchat with your client because being coffee-worthy isn't something you can pull off based on a script. Let's face it; if you are incapable of starting a conversation with a prospect, I can't help you!

Make it your goal to be deemed "coffee-worthy" within the first three minutes of the conversation.

But if your mindset is right, if you approach the conversation with intentionality, if you are committed to being as coffee-worthy as you know how to be—you'll be there!

I recommend starting off your client meeting with at least 30 seconds in coffee-worthy conversation. It can be longer than that, but I encourage you to let your clients decide. Remember, the purpose of this time is to build a foundation of trust that will lead to asking your first discovery questions.

Application Break

- Make a list of the characteristics that would make you "coffee-worthy." Then apply that list to your opening conversations. What, specifically, can you do to promote this opinion with your new prospect?

STARTING THE CONVERSATION

The opening conversation with new clients should be organic, flowing naturally in the moment. That said, when you meet someone for the first time at an open house or in a model home, it can feel anything but natural. So having a "go-to" opening question or conversation starter is essential. Have it "at the ready" for when the door suddenly swings open and you need to get a conversation started in a hurry.

Here are several "starter" questions that might help you develop an instinctive "go-to" conversation opener. Note that they all serve as relationship foundation questions.

- Any question regarding the weather. (That's why God made weather—so that salespeople can start a conversation!)

- Any question that allows for personalization (a car, sweatshirt, bumper sticker—anything that promotes a connection).

- *"How is your day going so far?"*

- *"Thanks for stopping by. Are you having a good day?"*

- *"So you're out shopping for a home. How's that going for you?"*

- *"How goes the home shopping? Are you having fun?"*

NOTE: The following are NOT relationship questions:

- *"What brought you out today?"*

- *"How did you find us?"*

- *"Is this your first time here?"*

- *"Are you in the market for a home?"*

These questions go *against* our principle of relationship building. They imply you're more interested in talking about the sale than in building the foundation for a Trust relationship.

Application Break

- Do you have a "go-to" rapport-building question? Try experimenting with different approaches to the greeting. It keeps you fresh and makes you sound more interesting. Overusing the same approach can make it all sound canned to the prospect.

PERMISSION TO QUESTION

So many salespeople struggle with what can be the awkward transition between building rapport and discovery. In fact, many get so into connecting with their client, they're at a loss as to how to bring the conversation back to business without losing the comfort and trust they'd just worked so hard to build.

I've got a solution for that. It's a technique called "Permission to Question," and it serves as an effective bridge between rapport building and discovery. By practicing this powerful tool with each of your clients in the rapport and discovery phase, you'll find it becomes second nature and your discussions will flow smoother and more productively.

Here's how it works. When you believe you have built the needed rapport, say to your client:

> *Asking permission to question is inherently respectful, and it sends a message that you're acting in your client's best interest right from the start.*

"Can I ask you a few quick questions so I can lead you in the right direction?"

Simple, yes? Indeed. Simple—and incredibly powerful!

Let's break it down. Let me share the key components of the "permission question."

- *"Can I . . . " (or "May I. . . " if you're a stickler for good grammar)*

What are you trying to communicate here? Respect. One of a prospect's greatest fears is that a salesperson will take control of the conversation against the will of the client. Asking permission says to the person, "You call the shots." By doing this, you put people at ease, allowing them to open up their comfort zone to you, not the other way around.

- *". . . a few quick questions . . . "*

I'm trying to let clients know this process will be painless and won't take long. They can get very uncomfortable when they don't know where the conversation is headed. Further, many clients are highly conscientious of their time. This way, you're letting them know you value their time and won't be taking up their entire afternoon.

- *". . . so that . . ."*

I want to communicate that this is for the *client*, not for *me*. I can serve clients best when I know them best. This shows you're genuinely interested in them.

(For more on the power of this question, I recommend reading Cialdini's book *Influence*. Focus on the principles of commitment and consistency.)

When you ask for permission to ask questions, your clients will say "yes" the overwhelming majority of the time, assuming you have a rapport in place. That's a critically important assumption, and it explains why we start the 4:2 progression with rapport building. But if you do this right, you put those clients into a position of being willing to answer just about any question you ask them.

Considering that position, I suggest it would be a good time to ask them the most important question in sales.

Which is the Motivation Question in the next chapter.

STUDY QUESTIONS:

1. Have you read Robert Cialdini's book *Influence: The Psychology of Persuasion?* If not, at least skim it or listen to a free podcast on iTunes University. Then do the self-assessment presented there. What are your persuasion strengths and weaknesses?

2. Jot down five or six of the typical conversation starters you use with potential clients. Now look at them critically; are they relationship questions? If not, how could you improve them for better relationship building?

3. Why would YOU want to have coffee with YOU? How could you make yourself even more coffee-worthy?

Chapter Sixteen:
Discovery Category #2:
Motivation Questions

By now, you probably realize there's nothing more important to learn about your clients than why they are moving in the first place. Their motivation tells a lot about so many areas of their life, especially when it is coupled with "tell me more about that" and other probing questions.

Consider this exchange between a salesperson and a client:

> *"Life is a series of collisions with the future; it is not the sum of what we have been, but what we yearn to be."*
>
> **Jose Ortega y Gasset**

Salesperson:	*"Tell me why you're wanting to move in the first place."*
Client:	*"Our home is too large, and we're thinking about downsizing."*

Salesperson:	*"Tell me more about that. What's changed?"*
Client:	*"Well, our kids are gone and we have a three-thousand-square-foot home. It's just the two of us now and we find ourselves doing a lot more traveling than before. We don't need a large home; we need more of a place to crash but something that's still big enough for grandkids down the road."*
Salesperson:	*"It sounds like a wonderful time in your life. Are you enjoying being empty nesters?"*
Client:	*"We miss our kids, but we love the independence. We also appreciate that if we can find a three-bedroom home at under $200,000, we'll be able to pay cash and not have a mortgage."*

Consider that the salesperson didn't ask a single "what"-based question. Everything was "why"-based and open-ended. So, what did she discover about her buyer?

- Motivation for moving
- Approximate size of the home
- Bedroom count
- Price point
- Interests
- Family information
- Desire for financial freedom

Look at that list! That's more than most salespeople determine in 20 minutes! Oh, and one more thing—that entire dialogue took just 30 seconds!

As you've noticed, when you ask the right question and you lead with a "why," you'll discover the motivation early on and shorten the presentation dramatically. That means less frustration for you, more time saved on the clients' end, and you get to the close more quickly.

Now, don't just think that you can swoop in and hit your clients over the head straight on with asking the motivation question right off the bat. The key to asking the Motivation Question is asking it conversationally. That's right—it has to sound like a part of the conversation. If it sounds like an interrogation, you're sunk. Your clients will feel cornered, as if they're no longer in control. If it sounds like you're reading from a script, forget it.

> *The key to asking the Motivation Question is to ask it conversationally and casually.*

You have to ask the question as if you had run into a friend from high school at the grocery school. And that means practice. Practice until it's so natural, it sounds like you're asking it for the very first time. Practice until it's so ingrained in you, you don't have to think about the question. You are free to interact with the clients, noting the nuances of their responses and seeking to understand the deeper messages behind them.

Here are sample Motivation Questions to get you started in developing the phrasing that works best for you:

- *"So why are you thinking about moving?"*
- *"So you're out shopping for a home. What got you thinking that it might be time to move?"*
- *"What was it that triggered your home search?"*

- *"What has you out shopping for a home?"*

- *"What has you in the market for a new home?"*

Application Break

- Practice, practice, and practice some more this three-step process: 1) Rapport-building; 2) Permission to Question; 3) Motivation Question. Get those down pat; they need to be absolutely seamless. Of course, it's best to practice with others before you begin to implement the technique with clients.

The final section of this book lays out a practice regimen strictly for this portion of the sales process. This practice regimen will walk you through the simple progression of:

✓ Trust-Building conversation

✓ Permission to Question

✓ Motivation Question with follow-ups ("Tell me more...")

I cannot emphasize enough the importance of getting this three-part opening down solid, buried deep into your unconscious competence. Remember, you're like an actor learning his lines; you must live and breathe your character, learning it inside and out. If you sound like you're scripted, if you sound like you're strained, if you stutter or stumble or in any way show a lack of confidence, you're hosed.

I don't know about you, but I'm excited! Here we are, not two minutes into the conversation and already we've established ourselves as coffee-worthy while learning vitally important pieces of information about our client. Whoever said that sales had to be painful?

Make this an enjoyable process for both you and your client, and you'll be well on your way to becoming a Trusted Advisor.

But there are a couple other things you need to know first—discussed in the next chapter.

STUDY QUESTIONS:

1. Closed questions that can be answered with yes or no tend to close off discussions. Open-ended questions like "why?" and requests like "tell me more" draw out more and deeper information and build the relationship. Make a list of five closed questions you have used in the past and then convert them into "tell me more" and "why?" questions.

2. Test the closed and open questions you listed with friends or family members. What do you observe?

3. How does this approach to questioning improve things for you and for your clients?

Chapter Seventeen:
Discovery Category #3:
Current Dissatisfaction

You know about the so-called tire-kickers out there—those people who will never purchase and just waste your time. This might come as a surprise, but I don't believe in any such thing. In fact, I believe that labeling a prospect as a "tire-kicker" gives me a convenient excuse for why I didn't sell them a home.

> *"Dissatisfaction with possession and achievement is one of the requisites to further achievement."*
>
> **John Hope**

Here's the deal: by virtue of the fact that people visited your website, or called you, or showed up in your office—trust me, they are legitimate prospects. How can I be sure of this fact? Because of an important principle: *There is no such thing as a perfect home.* Today, they're living in a flawed home. They've contacted your office to do something about it.

Understand this: everyone compromises. Everyone. Even Bill Gates compromised on the last home he purchased. Don't believe me?

With the last home he bought, he had to compromise on the size of the lot. The fact is, they wouldn't let him buy a whole country!

Everyone has to compromise because the absolutely perfect home doesn't exist. In fact, you compromised when you first acquired the home you're in right now. Don't tell me there are people out there who have no Dissatisfaction. It might be a low level of satisfaction, but there's always something.

It's that Dissatisfaction that drives clients through our doors. If everything were perfect in the home they live in today, they wouldn't be here (as discussed in Sections 1 and 2, remember?).

Buying a home involves a certain degree of psychological compromise. The job of the sales professional is to determine the "acceptable level of Dissatisfaction." That term defines the way that the homebuyer copes with his or her expectations. (Note: you probably don't want to use the phrase "acceptable level of Dissatisfaction" in a sales presentation!)

If you'd like an illustration of this principle, watch one episode of House Hunters on HGTV. See if the narration doesn't start this way:

"Jack and Barbara have outgrown their two-bedroom apartment. It was perfect when it was just the two of them, but when their fourth child came along, they knew they had to move. Jack and Barbara are in the market for a seven-bedroom, 8,000 square-foot home with a view of the ocean and twenty groomed acres, and their budget is $200,000."

OK, so it's not that dramatic, but you get the picture. The key is to watch the *end* of the show and see what they bought. I guarantee you it is *nothing* like what they said they wanted! Chances are, Jack and Barbara found their "acceptable level of Dissatisfaction" in a four-bedroom ranch with a finished basement and a modest backyard. No, they won't be grooming ponies on the property, but the home fits their needs and their budget, and their kids can even get a dog.

Why are they excited about something that fell so far short of their initial description? Because everyone compromises. Everyone.

Now what happens? Well, the longer people stay in their home, the more that Dissatisfaction rises (as discussed in Section 1). When the Dissatisfaction they feel is high enough, they come through your door—that's just the way it works.

> *Buying a home forces people to determine their acceptable level of Dissatisfaction.*

Your job as a Trusted Advisor is to identify those areas of Dissatisfaction by asking your client open-ended questions about what's wrong right now. Too many salespeople gloss over this part of the process; they're too eager to whip up a list of properties and whisk the clients out of their office and into an open house. Don't you see? These salespeople are doing nothing more than spinning their wheels! There's no solution if there isn't first a problem identified!

Here's what you need to find out before you can even consider finding your prospects a list of properties:

- What's wrong with the home they're in now?
- Why can't they stay there?
- What would they change if they were going to stay?
- What causes them frustration and angst?

Here are some questions that might help you get there:

- *"What is it that you really don't like about the home you're in now?"*
- *"What will you be happy to leave behind when you move?"*
- *"What causes you frustration in your current home?"*
- *"Is there anything about your home right now that embarrasses you when guests come over?"*
- *"If you had thirty thousand dollars to spend on fixing up the home you're in now, where would you spend it?"*

Application Break

- Determine your most powerful Dissatisfaction Question and incorporate it into your sales presentation immediately. Commit to following up with "Tell me more about that" every single time.

Now, keep in mind, there are two important things to know in our discussion on Current Dissatisfaction:

1) Sometimes the buyer's Motivation and Current Dissatisfaction are one and the same. For example, if you ask a couple why they're thinking about moving, they might just tell you that they hate their home, that they've outgrown the space, and that they can't move soon enough. That answer encompasses both Motivation and Current Dissatisfaction. If that's the case, be sure to pay attention to point #2.

2) It's about the why behind the "why." You can't fully understand the clients' Current Dissatisfaction until you understand it on an emotional level. People don't move because of their Dissatisfaction; they move because of the *pain* associated with their Dissatisfaction. I can't emphasize enough just how important it is to understand the emotional impact of your clients' Current Dissatisfaction.

When working with your clients it is imperative that you resist the temptation to move too quickly into what the clients want. By understanding the Current Dissatisfaction well enough, you'll also understand the Future Promise to a large extent.

Speaking of which…

STUDY QUESTIONS:

1. If you start showing homes to clients before you understand their Current Dissatisfaction, what will the impact be for your clients and for you?

2. Why is it valuable to go deeper than mere Dissatisfaction to truly understand the clients ' pain?

3. Current Dissatisfaction generally gets greater over time. How can you discuss this with clients to help them be ready to act on their Dissatisfaction sooner rather than later?

Chapter Eighteen:
Discovery Category #4:
Future Promise

Now, we've seen the first three steps of the sales process: Relationship, Motivation, and Current Dissatisfaction. Only when we have fully understood and internalized these steps can we effectively reach step four: Future Promise.

> *"The future belongs to those who believe in the beauty of their dreams."*
>
> **Eleanor Roosevelt**

The Future Promise encompasses the solution to their problem. Remember how Nido Qubein put it ever so eloquently: "People don't buy products. They buy the solutions that the products represent."

The Future Promise that you've helped outline for your clients represents their dream, their vision. That is what awaits them on the other side of the process of buying a home. The Future Promise is the light at the end of the tunnel for your homebuyers.

Determining the Future Promise is critical because it opens you up to an amazing depth of knowledge about your clients' hopes and dreams. You have to understand, your prospects have been thinking about their Future Promise for months, maybe even years. Why do you think magazines like *Better Homes and Gardens* and shows like *House Hunters* exist? They fuel the Future Promise.

Homebuilders construct model homes and hire interior designers to deck them out in high fashion in order to show the prospective buyers what their Future Promise might look like. A home stager creates a dream home out of an ordinary A-frame. That's all about maximizing the Future Promise. In short, if your clients can't come away with a clear vision of the Future Promise—no sale.

As a sales professional, it is your responsibility—no, it is your *duty*—to not only identify the Future Promise, but also understand *why* the clients desire such things. Without this, you are doing yourself and your clients a huge disservice.

> *"People don't buy products; they buy the solutions that the products represent."*
>
> **Nido Qubein**

And here we are—back to the "why."

It's not enough that clients want four bedrooms. How they live their lives is what really counts: a spare room for company, separate bedrooms for the kids, a home office for Mom. It's the flexibility they experience with the added space.

It's not enough that clients want a large yard. It's what that large yard represents: getting a dog for the kids, grilling out during the 4th of July, inviting the family over for their son's graduation. It's the freedom to enjoy time with their family and be able to have the things they want.

Even the location is a massively subjective variable. Some folks want nothing more than the peace and quiet of a country lifestyle while others may want a fast-paced environment with everything in walking distance. What might be a killer location to you may not be to me, and vice versa.

Often, the Future Promise becomes obvious by simply looking at the Current Dissatisfaction. But what about those clients for whom the Current Dissatisfaction is initially not that strong? Remember, a compelling Future Promise can actually *create* Current Dissatisfaction.

When they see how wonderful their lives can be, they also reflect on what they have now. It causes them to start comparing their lives and what they have to what they don't. Suddenly, the homebuyers realize they have been missing out.

I remember walking the exhibit floor at the International Builder Show and seeing an interesting display. A lighting company had set up a bed in their display area to demonstrate their product.

Here's how it worked. Suppose it's three in the morning and you have to get up to do what you do at three in the morning. Under the carpet next to the bed is a sensor that picks up the fact that you have stood up in the middle of the night in a dark bedroom. At this point, low-level lights go on to illuminate the baseboards from your bed to your bathroom.

Did you just have the same impression I had? I thought, "That's the coolest thing I've ever seen in my life." But what was the basis for my enthusiasm? Three years ago, I absolutely crushed my big toe on a doorjamb walking around in the middle of the night. I mean to tell you, I dropped onto the bathroom floor in agony. It is still a painful memory.

> *Sometimes a compelling Future Promise creates a Dissatisfaction in the prospect's mind.*

After that episode, I thought I'd solved the problem by installing a motion detector nightlight. It proved to be an adequate fix, except that it was glaringly bright and stayed on for too long, small annoyances compared to slamming my toe again. My Current Dissatisfaction had subsided—until I saw an amazing Future Promise. Suddenly I hated my night-light, and my Current Dissatisfaction soared all over again.

Application Break

- How would you phrase the perfect Future Promise question? Practice several different questions out loud and determine what sounds right for your style. Then work these questions into your presentation as soon as possible (don't forget the "Tell me more about that"!).

MUST-HAVES VS. WOULD-LIKE-TO-HAVES

The Future Promise is about identifying your clients' ideal. Remember, they all have two lists in their heads:

1. The "Must-Haves"
2. The "Would-Like-To-Haves"

Don't be dissuaded by clients with Future Promises that are initially too high. Remember, there's no such thing as perfect. The clients will compromise—they have to. Everyone does.

Make sure, though, that you have delineated between what the clients must have and what they would like to have before moving to the next step. As I mentioned earlier, many salespeople want to move straight to the show and tell.

Here are some sample questions that will help you develop the perfect phrasing for your own Future Promise questions:

- *"What are some of the "must-haves on your list?" ("And what else?")*

- *"What are some of the things about your old home that you'd bring over to your new one if you could?"*

- *"What have you seen that you really like?"*

- *"Describe some of the elements of your dream home."*

- *"Are there certain areas of the home that are important to you? Describe your ideal area."*

- *"Describe what a great Saturday morning would look like in your new home."*

STUDY QUESTIONS:

1. How will you help clients with unrealistic "must-haves" accept a subset of their starting list—and be delighted?

2. Just as we asked "why" to understand the pain of the Current Dissatisfaction, we ask "why" again to understand the deeper elements of the Future Promise. Why is it important to understand the passion that drives these needs?

3. How does helping the clients articulate a Future Promise make the whole homebuying process more effective and more enjoyable for both the clients and you?

Chapter Nineteen:
The Summary Questions

Up to this point, we've covered a new way of structuring the discovery process. The goal? To maximize our understanding of the clients' mission to improve their lives. Now, the question is: what do we do with it?

It's one thing to have great information; it's another to be able to leverage it properly. But that's precisely what separates the real pros from the amateurs.

Here's what usually happens with a book like this: the majority of salespeople will cherry-pick the parts they like from what they've read so far and attempt to apply it. A small minority will embrace the four discovery categories and use them as part of their sales technique. However, it's in The Summary Questions where a select few will

> *"Don't make assumptions. Find the courage to ask questions… Communicate with others as clearly as you can to avoid misunderstanding, sadness and drama. With just this one agreement, you can completely transform your life."*
>
> **Miguel Angel Ruiz**

stand apart. They'll be the ones who use this tool to its fullest potential.

I want to suggest that The Summary Questions I will show you have the potential to completely revolutionize your sales presentation. They are exceedingly powerful questions that will take your sales game to an entirely new level. More important—and I assure you this happens if you do it properly—*your clients will love you for it!*

The Summary Questions are comprised of two questions that come directly after your four Discovery Categories (hence The 4:2 Formula). You can't do the "2" without the "4." You have to get the Discovery Categories down first. Without those, you have only half of the story; it's like trying to put a roof on a house when you haven't built the walls yet.

The Summary Questions start with a clear understanding of the clients' mission. Remember, they're on a mission to improve their lives. They want their kids to be safe. They want neighbors they like. They want a home they're not embarrassed to show to their friends and co-workers. They want the freedom, flexibility, and peace of mind that comes with whatever their Future Promise holds for them.

They want you to show them how their lives will improve.

When I've discovered the clients' mission, it's time to rephrase that back to them in the form of closing/agreement questions. You see, I want the clients to agree—not with me, **but with themselves.** The clients need to acknowledge internally how their lives will improve.

> *The Summary Questions start with a clear understanding of the clients' mission.*

The Summary Questions do just that.

These two questions (the "2" of the "4:2") make for a powerful summation of the conversation at this point, and they direct the remainder of the sales process.

There are two Summary Questions:

1. The Summary Dissatisfaction Question
2. The Summary Solution Question

I like to call these "Summary Questions" because they summarize everything I've learned from the clients. They summarize their experience, pain, fear, hopes, and dreams succinctly and effectively.

There are three compelling advantages to using The Summary Questions:

1. They bring clarity of thought to your clients, helping them to focus on what really matters.
2. They prove your interest in understanding. As the salesperson, you're recounting what you have heard and confirming you heard correctly. Most salespeople never do this, but you'll find it's most welcome and greatly appreciated by a client.
3. They lock in place both the Current Dissatisfaction and the Future Promise, and they demand an action response. The clients agree with *themselves* that action must be taken.

Here's how these two questions work—shown in the next chapter.

STUDY QUESTIONS:

1. Why would clients appreciate the Summary Question process? What value does it add for them?

2. Why are clients more motivated to take action after the Summary Question process?

Chapter Twenty:
Summary Question #1:
The Summary Dissatisfaction
Question (SDQ)

The first of The Summary Questions is called the "Summary Dissatisfaction Question," and the name fits quite well. With this question, I recap the clients' pain and confirm why change is necessary. For example, I can say to them:

> "A prudent question is one-half of wisdom."
>
> **Francis Bacon**

"Let me make sure I'm clear—if you stay where you are, you will be living in a home that you have clearly outgrown, your children will be in a school you're not thrilled about, and your maintenance bills will continue to increase. Do I have that right?"

Let me break that down.

I simply recalled what I had learned from the discovery phase and fed it back in simple language. I'm not making anything up, and I'm not embellishing. I'm simply paraphrasing what the clients told me and repeating it back to them. This shows them I have been actively listening. If I did my homework and asked for the "why behind the why," I understand the problem in emotional terms. This technique simply recounts that; it confirms to the clients that staying put is not an option.

> *The Summary Dissatisfaction Question rephrases all that is wrong with the clients' current situation. It recaps their mission – how their life needs to improve.*

The structure of the question is as follows:

1. Begin the summary. I used the phrase, *"Let me make sure I'm clear on this—"* as a way to communicate we are resetting. You don't have to say these exact words; choose the language that works best for you.

2. *"If you stay where you are—"* The key is to direct them back to what was wrong *before* they met you. It's not about what they miss out on if they don't move forward—it's about why they are in the market in the first place, about what needs to improve.

3. *"You'll have to put up with—"* I want my clients to feel the pain, discomfort, and distaste in staying put. I'm not trying to be manipulative here; after all, it was that very Dissatisfaction that brought them to me in the first place. I'm just feeding back what's already inside.

4. (*List the Items*) Simply list the key reasons why their current situation is not right. Be careful not to phrase this in terms of what they'll miss out on if they don't move forward—that comes from The Summary Solution Question. (We'll get to that.)

5. *"Did I get that right?"* Remember, this is a CLOSING question. It's not enough to just state it. Clients have to *agree* with it! Also note that there's a hard stop here before I move to The Summary Solution Question. I need to see the clients' heads nod once or twice.

If you do your job right, you'll find that your clients won't only acknowledge your accuracy but also appreciate that you were listening, and that you understand them.

Application Break

- Recall two clients to whom you recently sold a home. If you could go back in time and place yourself at that moment in the discovery process where you had adequately determined their Dissatisfaction, how might you have asked this Summary Dissatisfaction Question? What would you have drawn out of their previous situation that proved the Dissatisfaction to be sufficiently elevated?

- If you can learn to do this on the fly—inserting the question at the tail end of the discovery period—you'll find a tremendous connection with your clients. Moreover, you'll find the clients agreeing with *themselves* that their Dissatisfaction is quite high.

BONUS OPPORTUNITY FOR TOP PROS

At times, you'll find that your clients' Dissatisfaction is quite high—so high, in fact, that staying put is not an option.

For example, let's suppose that these prospects come into your sales office because of ongoing crime in the area where they live. Let's further suppose that there was a shooting yesterday on the next street over. This incident constituted a "last straw" moment for your prospects.

In a case when the Dissatisfaction is sky-high, I don't actually need to ask a Summary Dissatisfaction Question. Rather, I can offer this in the form of an assumptive statement.

For example, *"Wow. That's really tough. So it sounds like staying put just isn't an option for you, is it?"*

As soon as the clients agree that staying put isn't an option, they've also agreed that they're moving somewhere. More than half the sale is already made at that point.

Look for those opportunities to make The Summary Dissatisfaction Question more of an assumptive statement, especially when you suspect the Dissatisfaction is extremely high.

STUDY QUESTIONS:

1. Recount the five elements of The Summary Dissatisfaction Question. Identify what could happen if you left out one of the steps? (Go through the five steps and identify the impact from each.)

2. Why is it important not to bring in some of the Future Promise information at this point?

3. How is The Summary Dissatisfaction Question a closing step?

Chapter Twenty-One:
Summary Question #2:
The Summary Solution Question
(SSQ)

Immediately after The Summary Dissatisfaction Question is asked and answered, we come right back with The Summary Solution Question. This is a recap of the most important things your clients are looking for, presented in an exciting, promising manner.

Note that the question is asked immediately after the clients have agreed to The Summary Dissatisfaction Question. Think "bang-bang" in your technique. The clients just solidified the pain in their own minds; now add the pleasure.

> *"To come to be you must have a vision of Being, a Dream, a Purpose, a Principle. You will become what your vision is."*
>
> **Peter Nivio Zarlenga**

The question sounds like this:

"So I need to find you something that offers a bedroom for each of your children PLUS a quiet office space, a drop-dead gorgeous kitchen, preferably with granite countertops and stainless appliances, ample closet space in the master, and a spacious yard that will work for two large dogs, all in the Wilsonville School District—did I get that right?"

Again, I'll break it down:

1. *"So I need to show you something that offers . . ."* This is not the oft-asked *"If I could show you . . . "* This is a promise you're making to them, not a commitment you're asking of them.

2. *". . . quiet . . . drop-dead gorgeous . . . ample . . . spacious . . . "* You want to use descriptive words that speak elegantly about the ideal picture. Make it dramatic and lift the tone of your voice!

3. *"Did I get that right?"* Again, this is a *closing* question. You need to see the prospects' heads nod north and south! And when they do, they have confirmed the clarity in their own mind. We have painted the picture; now all we need to do is find that house!

Note: The Summary Solution Question is not an "If I could, would you?" question, as is taught in many training formats. With all due respect to other trainers, I'm not a fan of this type of question. (That doesn't make me right but bear with me while I present my case.) The "If I could, would you?" technique can be seen as manipulative by an increasingly skeptical prospect. With this approach I am, in effect, asking a client to make a commitment on a concept. (*"If I could ... "*)

Not only is that technique potentially dangerous, I'm not sure it's necessary. If my clients have already agreed with me on my questions, then they have closed themselves in advance anyway.

Think about it: all I have to do now is show them what I just agreed to show them. When I do that, they'll have already admitted that a) they can't stay where they are, and b) I have what they are looking for. What about that is *not* putting me in a position to close?

Application Break

- This might be the most important application point of all. Practice The Summary Questions over and over and over again. Practice with no interruption between the two questions. As soon as the client agrees with The Summary Dissatisfaction Question, immediately ask The Summary Solution Question. There can be no pause and no hesitation. Think "bang-bang" in how you ask.

THE HOLY GRAIL OF DISCOVERY: MUTUAL PURPOSE

When you have completed The 4:2 Formula, you're doing more than nailing down the discovery of your clients' Current Dissatisfaction. You will have reached the most coveted of positions—that of Trusted Advisor. Only a few minutes into the conversation you will have achieved mutual purpose.

Mutual purpose is the end-all, the signal, that you're on the same team and striving for the same goal. Most

> *Mutual purpose is the end-all, the signal, that you're on the same team and striving for the same goal.*

salespeople never reach this point with their clients. That's why they continually feel as if making a sale is like playing a tug-of-war with their clients. Mutual purpose involves positioning yourself as a Trusted Advisor. It's the surest sign you're on the same page with your clients.

Together now, you will seek the solution, and you will do so as partners. How great is that?

Mutual purpose is the ultimate goal, but it requires several components to be in place, which we've already addressed including:

> ➤ Rapport and Trust; Likability (coffee-worthy)
> ➤ Understanding of Buyer's Motivation (on a deep level)
> ➤ Knowing the Current Dissatisfaction
> ➤ Knowing the Future Promise
> ➤ Summarizing the Dissatisfaction
> ➤ Summarizing the Solution

STUDY QUESTIONS:

1. What are the three elements of The Summary Solution Question?

2. Have you ever felt that you've achieved mutual purpose with a client? How did you feel? What was different about that search and selling experience vs. others that were not close to achieving mutual purpose?

3. As review, list the six items in The 4:2 Formula. Did you get them all? Now memorize them!

Chapter Twenty-Two:
Filling In the Information Gaps

If you've been paying close attention, you'll notice we missed a few minor details along the way, things like:

- ✓ Price Point
- ✓ Square Footage
- ✓ Time Frame
- ✓ Financing Capability
- ✓ Bedroom Count

Wow. Aren't these important things to have left out of a book that focuses on knowing your client? Stay with me; this will make perfect sense when I'm done.

By no means am I suggesting that the details in the checklist are not important; nothing could be further from the truth. Rather, the focus is on tim-

> *"Normally I work out a general summary of what I mean to do, then start writing, and the details can be different from my anticipation. So there is considerable flow, but always within channels."*
>
> **Piers Anthony**

ing—that is, *when* is the right time to determine those things?

I contend that if you follow the 4:2 Formula, something amazing will happen. You'll learn those things without having to ask the questions! So often the "why" questions will lead you to the "what" answers.

Of course, it doesn't always happen that way, so you need to be prepared to ask some fill-in-the-gap questions after you've finished the 4:2 process. The key is in the technique. I propose a method of making those detail questions much easier for the client to answer.

Suppose you walk into a car dealership. You had previously decided you would spend up to $30,000 for a new car. The salesperson approaches and immediately asks, "What is the most you are willing to spend?" If you are like most car buyers, you will probably answer something like, "$27,500." Why would you bald-faced lie like that? Because it is a difficult question to answer. You'd Fear that you were putting yourself at a disadvantage.

> *I propose a method of making those detail questions much easier for the client to answer.*

Now let's suppose the car salesperson asked about why you needed a car first and *then* about what you were looking for. Suppose the sales professional was mission-oriented and completely coffee-worthy. Five minutes into the presentation, the salesperson says, "The car I want to show you offers (list of features) and it sells for $29,500. Is that in the price range you were hoping for?"

See the difference? In the second approach, the sales professional makes it much easier to answer the question. This is *exactly* the technique I suggest you use.

Here's how it works: Once you've learned what you need to know about the client's mission (using the four discovery categories) and established mutual purpose with the prospect (using The Summary Questions), complete this portion of the conversation by describing what you want to show them and asking if the details will work for them.

Instead of asking, *"How many bedrooms are you looking for?"* say, *"Based on what you've told me I have a home I definitely want to show you. It has four bedrooms and is about twenty-three hundred square feet. Is that what you were hoping to find?"*

Instead of asking their price point, say, *"The home is priced at $275,800. Does that sound like the price range you were hoping to find?"*

Instead of asking for their time frame, ask, *"The home can be ready for move-in in sixty days. Will that work for your schedule?"*

Note that I am only using this technique to fill in the gaps of missing information. If I did the 4:2 properly, I'd probably already know these things!

Application Break

- Practice *not* asking typical questions that are regularly asked in sales conversations (e.g., bedroom count, time frame, price point, etc.) during the first five minutes of the conversation. Just get to know the client using the 4:2 process and see if you don't learn all that you need anyway.

So, there you have it, The 4:2 Formula, the key to uncovering your clients' Current Dissatisfaction and delivering their Future Promise. There's no other sales method quite like it. But you have to be willing to apply it.

The rest of this book will help you to do just that. With that in mind, let's take a look at the 10-week guide to successfully implementing The 4:2 Formula next...

SECTION 4:

THE 10-WEEK STUDY GUIDE TO 4:2 SELLING

Let's Get To Work . . .

All right, my friends. You've made it this far. Now let's get this kicked into productive application. My job is to give you the education; your job is to use it in your sales environment. It doesn't matter what the consultant puts on the page; the only thing that counts is what you decide to put into action!

To get started, I'm making a strange recommendation. Please reread 10 segments of the book, this time at a much slower pace. Trust me, it will be way easier the second time. But more important, the results will be dramatically more powerful. Here's why.

Not unlike music, drama, athletics, dance, or even surgery, sales is a performance art. How does one attain mastery in a performance art? Your instinctive answer is probably "practice," and you are partially correct. But as stated previously, it's *repetition* that makes the real difference. A dancer performs the same move over and over again. An athlete takes part in the same drill dozens of times in a row. And if I'm having surgery, I would prefer to be under the care of a surgeon who has more than a few notches on his surgical belt.

Every time we repeat a behavior properly, we find that competency to be more deeply engrained into our subconscious. We make that behavior more automatic, more refined, and more polished. Moving toward unconscious competence comes only through repetition.

My challenge to you is to go back and read through 10 segments in 10 weeks, all the while taking the lessons to an entirely new depth. I will lay out that schedule for you here; your job is to commit to getting beyond "head" knowledge and build the repetitive mental muscle that locks the behavior deep into your psyche.

Three things will help you maximize this journey:

1. Be sure to journal throughout. Writing down your thoughts, progress, frustrations, questions, and so on will prove to be an invaluable effort. Journaling keeps you focused and allows you to measure your progress. There's a degree of self-accountability you'll experience by journaling. If you've never tried it, this is the perfect opportunity. We've given you plenty of space for that purpose in this book.

2. Find a practice partner. You can attempt to practice alone, but your progress will be dramatically improved by having a partner. Partners see things that you don't. They hold you accountable in your practice patterns. They can coach and encourage along the way. If you're looking to ramp up your performance more quickly, this is the way to do it.

3. Apply every day. You want to build in habits of constant performance improvement. This comes through daily practice and attention. If you put the project aside even for a couple of days, you'll notice immediate consequences. First, your aptitude will decline quickly. Second, your motivation will recede, making it harder to start again. Third, you'll be hesitant to actually attempt the techniques in a sales conversation. So make this a daily commitment.

WEEK 1: BUILD TRUST

- Reread Chapter 15 on Trust Building.

- Make a list of the "coffee-worthy" attributes you wish to project. Share that list with others and solicit their input.

Coffee-Worthy Attributes:

✓ _____

✓ _____

✓ _____

✓ _____

✓ _____

✓ _____

- Practice your most fully engaged, positive-energy greeting. Make a decision to stand out in an instant. Practice good facial posture. Be 100% present.

Elements of My Perfect Greeting:

✓ _____

✓ _____

✓ _____

✓ _____

- Pay attention to how your initial coffee-worthy attitude is paying off as you extend the discussion with your prospects. Journal the difference that your attitude makes in the remainder of the conversation. Celebrate the victory.

_____

_____

_____

_____

_____

- Build the habit of strong positive energy right out of the gate. Write down a positive habit-forming statement and read it before every sales encounter.

_____

_____

_____

_____

WEEK 2: PERMISSION TO QUESTION

- Reread the section from Chapter 15 on the "Permission to Question" technique.

- Rewrite that question in your own words. Read it out loud several times to make sure it's exactly as you would say it in an actual conversation. Make sure the question covers these three messages you're attempting to convey to your prospect:

1. *"May I . . ."* (you, client, are in control)
2. *". . . a few quick questions . . ."* (this won't take long)
3. *". . . point you in the right direction?"* (this is for you, not for me)

_____

_____

_____

_____

- Practice asking that question out loud over and over again. Get it down so it's natural and conversational. Remember, it's best to practice with a partner for added accountability and faster results.

- Use the question five times this week with clients. Check a box each time you use this question.

1.	2.	3.	4.	5.

- Journal your progress. Write a brief statement on how you're doing so far. Celebrate your victories. Focus on progress each day.

_____

_____

_____

_____

_____

_____

WEEK 3: MOTIVATION

- Reread Chapter 16 on determining your prospects' motivation.

- Think back on the last three people you have sold a home to. Jot down their motivation, explaining how their lives needed to improve.

1. _____

_____

2. _____

_____

3. _____

_____

- Think through the most natural way to ask the Motivation Question, referring back to Chapter 16 for suggestions. Write out your ideal Motivation Question, saying it out loud as you go to make sure it sounds like you.

_____

_____

_____

_____

_____

- Practice the Motivation Question over and over. Do this dozens of times over several days. Practice until the question is automatic and conversational, until you don't have to think about it when you ask.

- Once the Motivation Question is down solid, practice by beginning with the "Permission to Question" (lesson from Week 2) and immediately transition into the Motivation Question without a pause.

- Use the question five times this week with clients. Check a box each time you use it.

1.	2.	3.	4.	5.

- Journal your results as you go along, paying particular attention to your comfort level in how you ask.

_____

_____

_____

_____

_____

_____

WEEK 4: "TELL ME MORE . . . "

- Reread Chapter 5, "The Why Behind the Why."

- Immediately begin to expand your curiosity skills by implementing this technique in your daily life. Use it in three non-sales conversations (either in your business life or in your personal/social life). Journal your results.

_____

_____

_____

_____

_____

_____

_____

_____

_____

_____

_____

_____

- Practice making the "Motivation" and the "Tell me more . . ." questions seamless—that is, assume a "tell me more" follow-up with every motivation question.

- Intentionally practice this "Tell me more . . ." technique on the heels of your Motivation Question with three clients this week.

- Journal your progress in using all three components: 1) Permission to Question; 2) Motivation Question; 3) "Tell me more . . ."

WEEK 5: CURRENT DISSATISFACTION

- Reread Chapter 17 on discovering Current Dissatisfaction.

- Think of the last home you purchased or rented. What was the Dissatisfaction in the *previous* situation that spurred your move? Write it down.

_____

_____

_____

- Think of three prospects you're working with today. List some aspects of their Current Dissatisfaction. Be sure you're stating these in emotional terms.

1. _____

   _____

2. _____

   _____

3. _____

   _____

- Write out your ideal Current Dissatisfaction question. As you write, say it out loud several times to ensure it's natural to your style.

  _____

  _____

  _____

- Use the exact Current Dissatisfaction question with three clients this week. Journal your efforts each time, adjusting to your greater effectiveness and celebrating your victories.

  _____

  _____

  _____

  _____

  _____

  _____

  _____

  _____

  _____

  _____

  _____

WEEK 6: FUTURE PROMISE

- Reread Chapter 18 on determining Future Promise.

- Think of the home you live in right now. Based on your Current Dissatisfaction, what are some key elements of Future Promise in your next home? Write them down.

✓ _____

✓ _____

✓ _____

✓ _____

✓ _____

✓ _____

- Think of three prospects you're working with today. List a few aspects of their Future Promise. Pay special attention to the emotional aspects; share what you think will bring them joy.

1. _____

_____

2. _____

_____

3. _____

_____

- Write out your ideal Future Promise question. As you write, say it out loud several times to ensure it's natural to your style.

  _____

  _____

  _____

  _____

- Use the exact Future Promise question with three clients this week. Journal their responses and evaluate your effectiveness.

  _____

  _____

  _____

  _____

  _____

  _____

WEEK 7: SUMMARY DISSATISFACTION QUESTION

- Reread Chapter 20, "The Summary Dissatisfaction Question."

- Think of the last people you sold a home to. If you were to have re-phrased their Current Dissatisfaction before you actually showed them a home, what would that question sound like? Be sure to follow the structure of a good Summary Dissatisfaction Question (*"If you stay where you're at, you'll have to put up with . . . Is that right?"*).

1. _____

   _____

2. _____

   _____

3. _____

   _____

- Think of three prospects you're working with today. Practice ways you could be asking The Summary Dissatisfaction Question. Use this as a repetition process, repeating the question over and over and improving each time.

1. _____

   _____

2. _____

   _____

3. _____

   _____

- Practice using The Summary Dissatisfaction Question three times this week. Journal your efforts each time, adjusting to your greater effectiveness and celebrating your victories.

  _____

  _____

  _____

  _____

  _____

  _____

- Remember that this is an advanced technique and, like any advanced technique, it takes time and repetition to perfect. Focus on your progress and celebrate every step.

WEEK 8: SUMMARY SOLUTION QUESTION

- Reread Chapter 21, "The Summary Solution Question."

- Think of the last people you sold a home to. If you were to have rephrased their Future Promise before you actually showed them a home, what would that question sound like? Be sure to follow the structure of a good Summary Solution Question ("*So I need to show you something that offers . . . Is that right?*").

  _____

  _____

  _____

  _____

- Think of three prospects you are working with today. Practice ways you could be asking The Summary Solution Question. Use this as a repetition process, repeating the question over and over and improving each time.

  1. _____

  _____

  2. _____

  _____

  3. _____

  _____

- Practice using The Summary Solution Question three times this week. Journal your efforts each time, adjusting to your greater effectiveness and celebrating your victories.

_____

_____

_____

_____

_____

_____

WEEK 9: FILLING IN THE INFORMATION GAPS

- Reread Chapter 22, "Filling in the Information Gaps."

- By now, you should be deferring on all those rote questions that everyone else asks right out of the gate (e.g., bedroom count, time frame, price range, etc.). If not, diligently force yourself to suspend those questions until after the 4:2 progression.

- Find a practice partner and go through the entire 4:2 progression at least three times. Ask the practice partner to come up with a different buyer profile each time. At the conclusion of each 4:2, use the techniques from Chapter 22 to fill in the information gap.

- Journal your results as you go.

_____

_____

_____

_____

_____

_____

_____

_____

_____

_____

_____

_____

WEEK 10: CELEBRATE YOUR VICTORY!

- Reread your journal notes going all the way back to Week 1 of your practice assignments. Celebrate the progress you've made along the way.

- Think back to your sales presentation before you started this journey. What are the three most significant changes in your approach, and how have they helped you become a better sales professional?

1. _____

   _____

2. _____

   _____

3. _____

   _____

- Read the stories of Ashley and Stephanie in the pages that follow. Based on what they say, how can you continue to improve your own performance going forward?

Appendix 1:
Success Stories

SUCCESS STORY #1:
ASHLEY HINESLEY, GOODALL HOMES, NASHVILLE, TN

You're a veteran salesperson. How has your selling style changed over the years?

When I started in sales, I was taught to ask the same questions I still hear from other salespeople: bedroom count, price range, time frame, and so on. But then you find yourself suggesting floor plans that fit the answers to those questions when you don't fully understand what's most important to the clients. Today, the most valuable piece of information I can find out is their motivation. Why they are moving in the first place?

Then I have an in-depth conversation that goes much deeper into their lives than I used to go. But I've learned that knowing *why* they are moving leads to a better alignment between my clients and me. As a result, we get to the right solution more quickly.

Why is that true?

I have so many homes I could show to my clients, and if all I knew was their bedroom count and price range, it would take forever to show them all. Let's face it: if I only knew they wanted four bedrooms at a price below $250,000, I wouldn't have a sense of where to start.

Now, I look to show them something that relates to their lives. I find out about their life situation today, and it tells me what they are moving *from*. Knowing that gives me clarity on what they are moving to.

What is the secret to that deeper discovery?

It's about leveraging the relationship and getting to know my clients on a deeper level. People are surprised at how much I can learn on the front end of the conversation. It gives me insights I would never have otherwise. And it leads me to interesting conversations and important information.

Are people hesitant to open up?

No, not if they believe I really care about them. I don't jump into the sales questions right away like I used to. Having this initial rapport-building time is critical in letting them know I care about them as people, not just whether they're going to buy a home from me. After that point, it's not difficult to get them to open up.

How are you standing out from the competitors?

I think I'm more memorable because I just don't sound like every other salesperson. At least that's what my clients tell me. Other salespeople are busy talking about their products; they don't really get into talking about the prospect's life.

Exactly which technique allows you to learn more in your conversation than your competitors do?

These days, I make a living off of one phrase: "Tell me more about that." In the past, I've wanted to rush forward to the solution, but I've learned that pausing and staying on a topic is not a bad thing at all.

Salespeople want to talk more than they should; that was always an issue for me in the past. I rushed to get to the product discussion quickly. It's still something I have to remember, but I have trained myself to go deeper to gain understanding. It makes all the difference in the world

Do you have an example of how you have used The 4:2 Formula with a recent homebuyer?

I was working with a couple who had been referred by their daughter. This older couple was moving from New York; their daughter lives here in Nashville. The father didn't want to open up right away, but he eventually stated he'd had a heart attack brought about by stress, largely from living in New York. I also discovered that the daughter was pregnant with yet another grandchild, and he was tired of living so far away from his grandkids.

The point is that this purchase was not about the home or the price or the lot size. It was all about how the couple could improve their lives!

There is a story behind every single person. I can one hundred percent say I have sold a lot of homes by getting to know my clients well.

SUCCESS STORY #2:
STEPHANIE SHARON, EASTWOOD HOMES, CHARLESTON, SC

How has your use of The 4:2 Formula changed the way you sell?

I've always believed in being sincere, and I've always had a desire to serve my clients. What I've learned through the 4:2 Formula is that I serve them best when I know them best. Now I spend a lot more time getting to know them on a deeper level.

I've always been a decent performer, but now I perform on a whole new plane. I've always had good client feedback surveys, but now the scores are off the charts. My sales have skyrocketed before I learned The 4:2 Formula. And now my sales have increased by fifty percent.

What are some examples of how your presentation style has changed?

The biggest change is what I hear from clients and even from other salespeople. I'm selling homes to people on the first day I meet them. Other Realtors are stunned at how quickly I can get people on contract. The biggest impact has been on how well I get to know my clients.

Give me an example of that.

I had a very, very grumpy couple come in looking for a home. From the start, they didn't want to talk to me, not even a little bit. It was just conversation like "give me a price sheet and let me walk around." I recognized from what I've learned about the 4:2 Formula that this is a symptom of their situation. These people aren't mean; they're just stressed out.

It turns out they had just driven 14 hours from Michigan for this house-hunting trip. And why? Because they recently suffered the loss of both of their dogs. These dogs were family members to this couple. Without them, they simply didn't want to stay in their home anymore. Also, because of the cold weather, they couldn't walk their dogs half the year. They wanted that to change with any future pets.

This couple purchased on the first day I met them, and by the end of the deal, we were like family. They were wonderful people. I had just met them when they were completely stressed out.

Are you seeing a shorter buying cycle now that you're using The 4:2 Formula?

It's dramatically shorter. Recently, a competitor came to me stunned that I had sold a couple a home on their first visit. The same people had told that salesperson they had a two-year time frame in mind. Bottom line, I get to know my clients more deeply and quickly than others do. That helps me solve their problems in a fraction of the time I could in the past.

How are you using The Summary Questions?

Those questions are absolutely essential to me. They prove to the clients that I have listened carefully, and that I really want to make sure I've got everything right. It is so powerful; they *love* it that I have listened.

I've found that The Summary Questions tie the pieces together. Asking them also gives my clients an opportunity to let me know if I missed something. It increases my efficiency so I can take them on the right path more quickly.

Do The Summary Questions increase your confidence?

Absolutely! Now I know I'm taking them to the right house right off the bat. I don't have to guess, and I don't have to show them a ton of homes. We get to the solution right away.

Do you have examples of what you learned using The 4:2 Formula?

Two examples come to mind. The first was a couple who said they were in no hurry. They showed no energy or urgency from the start. When I asked why they were moving, they said they were renting and wanted a change.

It took several different ways of my following up with "Tell me more about that" to get them to open up. Eventually, they told me their apartment was infested with cockroaches. Not only were they embarrassed about their living conditions, but they also felt like bad parents to their two year old.

When they came into my office, they were "just looking." They had no idea they could actually buy anything. But buy they did. The most amazing thing is that their telling me what was really going on gave me one of the best feelings ever. I knew immediately I was hearing things that were deep and personal to them—things they wouldn't share with just anyone.

Here's one other example that's personal to me. A dear friend's husband passed away last year. It was obviously a difficult time, particularly for my friend.

One thing she and her husband enjoyed about their place was the abundance of trees surrounding their home. So when she was looking for a new home during this difficult time, she wanted to get away from living among lots of trees. She found the idea depressing; it was a constant reminder of a life she could no longer have. But what do you think most salespeople talked about? Trees! They wanted to show her home sites with trees everywhere because they never bothered to discover her real issues.

That is really powerful. Any advice for new salespeople?

Most salespeople want to talk about the product. My advice is to get to know the people. You'll successfully determine the right product when you understand the people.

Appendix 2:
Sample Scripts

As you read through these sample scripts, look for the 4:2 pattern in the conversations. By now, you'll have a good understanding how the progression unfolds. It might be helpful to read the salesperson's lines out loud to get additional practice honing your delivery.

THE 4:2 FORMULA SAMPLE SCRIPT #1

(SP = Salesperson; C = Client)

SP: Good afternoon. I'm Robert. And you are?

C: Wayne and Marianne. How are you?

SP: Doing great. Thanks for asking. How's your day going?

C: It's fine. A little tiring, but we're getting by.

SP: House hunting can be tiring, no doubt. But do you enjoy the process?

C: I guess. It gets confusing after a while, but we're hanging in there.

SP: Absolutely. Well, thanks for stopping by here. I know you have a lot of choices on where you could have stopped. Thanks for including us on that list. Can I get you a bottled water?

C: We're fine, thanks.

SP: Well, I want to be able to point you in the right direction. Can I ask you a few quick questions?

C: Sure.

SP: Great. Let's start here: why are you thinking about moving in the first place?

C: Our place is way too small.

SP: Tell me more about that. What makes it way too small.

C: We have three boys ages ten, twelve, and fifteen. They're very active and always fighting. And I work out of my house, so it's just not a peaceful environment.

SP: So you need not only more space but a separation of space as well?

C: Yeah, that sounds right.

SP: Tell me about the home. What isn't working?

C: For one thing, it's only three bedrooms so two of the boys have to double up. Plus my office is in my master bedroom.

SP: And I take it that's not working out so well?

C: Especially when I have to make calls to a different time zone.

SP: Got it. What else would you like to improve?

C: The kitchen is old; it needs to be completely updated. It just screams 1980s. The backyard is a decent size, but we would like something bigger. The boys spend a lot of time in the yard. Also, the utility bills are ridiculously high due to poor insulation. In the winter, we walk past the windows and can feel the cold breeze.

SP: That's extremely helpful. Thanks. Now, what are some of the "must-have" items on your list?

C: A great kitchen with an island and all the things that modern kitchens come with: granite countertops, stainless steel, lots of cabinet space, an island . . .

SP: Okay. What else is on the list?

C: Well, we'd love to have a bonus room that's removed from the main living areas—a place where the boys can make all the noise they want. And it would be great if we could find a three-car garage.

SP: Tell me more about that.

C: We're at that age when the boys will be driving soon, and we're going to run out of space to park our cars.

SP: Anything else you're looking for?

C: We'd love to have a really nice master bathroom.

SP: What do you have now?

C: A coat closet with a toilet in it! Seriously, it's really small and outdated.

SP: Thanks for sharing all that with me. Let me see if I've got this straight. It sounds like if you stay where you're at, you'll be in a home that you have clearly outgrown, with three active boys who are making for a less-than-peaceful environment, a kitchen you're not particularly proud of, and a master bathroom that sounds like something from your first apartment. Did I get that right?

C: You nailed it.

SP: So staying put just isn't an option for you?

C: That's correct.

SP: Got it. So I need to show you something that complements your family in the way you live today. A great family room area that opens to the kitchen so you can be together when you want to be, but it has to have separate spaces for everyone; your own office tucked away from the common space; bedrooms for each of the boys; and a bonus room for the boys to escape to. And we want to see those great appointments that make a home so special: a drop-dead gorgeous kitchen with a large island and plenty of countertop space and a master bathroom you might find in a million-dollar home. Finally, you need a yard space that's big enough to let your boys be boys and a three-car garage. Did I get all that right?

C: That is absolutely right. We would love to find exactly that.

SP: Good news. I have something I definitely want to show you. The home is five bedrooms and has twenty-eight hundred square feet. Does that sound about right?

C: That'll work.

SP: The home is priced at $355,500. Does that meet your price range?

C: It's more than we wanted to spend, but we're willing to look at it.

SP: That home will be ready for move-in in ninety days. How does that work for your timing?

C: We're renting our home now, so we're flexible.

SP: Outstanding! Sounds like we've got a real possibility. Let's take a look!

THE 4:2 FORMULA SAMPLE SCRIPT #2

SP: Hi, there! How are you?

C: I'm good. Thanks.

SP: I'm Marcia.

C: My name is Cindy.

SP: Hi, Cindy. How's your day going?

C: It's fine. I'm a little rushed, but I'm getting through it all.

SP: Well, I can help you keep this as simple as possible. Can I ask you a few quick questions so I can point you in the right direction?

C: Certainly.

SP: Let's start here. What has you thinking it might be time to move?

C: I'm being relocated here from Denver.

SP: Oh, I see. How are you feeling about that? Excited? Scared?

C: A little of both. I was born and raised in Denver, so it will be hard to leave. But the job is right, and I'm looking forward to a new chapter in my life.

SP: That's wonderful, Cindy. Congratulations. Tell me about the home you're living in now. What do you like about it, and what do you not like?

C: I'm in a townhouse now and I really like it, except for the shared walls.

SP: Tell me more. What is it that concerns you?

C: I don't want to have to worry about playing my music too loud or about a fire starting in one unit and moving to another. And I'm just ready to have my own space.

SP: Got it. And what are some of the important aspects of your new home? What's on your wish list?

C: I need a big kitchen.

SP: Tell me more about that.

C: I love to cook, so I need a lot of countertop space for preparation. I also plan to entertain so I want to have a gathering place in the kitchen—an island.

SP: Do you have a big kitchen now?

C: I do, and I love it.

SP: OK. What else is important to you?

C: I play the piano, and I need space for that.

SP: That's awesome. I wish I played. How big is the piano, and how much space do you need?

C: It's a baby grand. Right now, it's in my formal dining space.

SP: And is that working out for you?

C: Yes, it's perfect.

SP: Okay, let me make sure I'm clear on this. This job relocation is a sure deal so staying put is not an option. You are moving, right?

C: Right.

SP: So to make this all work for you, we need to find the best of what you already have and combine it with what's lacking. That means a magazine-quality gourmet kitchen with all the bells and whistles; a detached home with your own yard and no neighbors to worry about; a defined space for your baby grand piano; and how about we include a master suite with a separate sitting area and a soaking tub in the bathroom?

C: That sounds perfect!

SP: I definitely have a couple of homes in mind. One in particular I think you're going to love. It's a three-bedroom home with a dramatic great room and a huge kitchen, and it's about eighteen hundred square feet. Sound good so far?

C: That sounds right to me.

SP: The home is basically ready for move-in today. Does that work?

C: The sooner the better.

SP: The home is priced at $279,900. Does that fit your price range?

C: Ouch. That's more than I was hoping to spend. Will the seller come down at all?

SP: Let me ask you this. Are we in the ballpark?

C: Yes, but it's just more than I had in mind.

SP: Fair enough. Let's take a look and see if you like it. If you don't like it, the price doesn't matter. But if you love it, then we can discuss the terms. Sound good to you?

C: Let's do it!

About the Author

Few sales leaders possess more extensive experience — and irresistible enthusiasm — than Jeff Shore. A voracious student of life and self-proclaimed sales "junkie," Jeff believes that sales is a noble profession and that salespeople who act in the best interest of their customers provide a valuable service to society.

Jeff began his residential real estate career in the 1980s as an agent for Coldwell Banker. Thriving in a tough market, Jeff further honed his craft during the California real estate downturn of the 1990s as an on-site new home sales counselor. During this time, Jeff moved quickly through a series of progressive sales management and executive positions for billion-dollar Fortune 500 homebuilder, KB Home. He later served in a corporate role as their National Sales Director, creating training programs, coaching managers, and directing sales strategy nationwide.

Today, Jeff provides sales strategy and training for sales organizations around the world, working with both executive and sales teams alike. Continually pressing for new levels of personal and professional performance, he delivers hard-hitting experiences that electrify teams with quick-witted humor, personal challenges, and relentless positivity.

An acclaimed member of the National Speakers Association and a regularly featured speaker at the International Builders Show, the Pacific Coast Builders Conference, and SMCs across the country, Jeff's coast-to-coast seminars garner ecstatic reviews from sales counselors and managers who describe them as "authentic," "entertaining," "inspiring," and "compelling." Speaking in front of thousands of sales professionals each year, Jeff remains one of the most popular speakers in the industry today.

When he's not on an airplane or working with sales teams, Jeff resides in Auburn, California with his wife Karen and their two dogs. Jeff and Karen find deep happiness spending time with their three grown children and enjoying friends, community and church activities and the overall small town life of their rural Northern California surroundings.

www.jeffshore.com | jeff@jeffshore.com

 facebook.com/JeffShoreCommunity

 @jeffshore

 youtube.com/jeffshoretraining

 Jeff Shore

BOOKING INFORMATION FOR KEYNOTES AND SEMINARS

Jeff Shore keeps his audience thinking, laughing and, most importantly, changing the way they do business. Seamlessly incorporating over two decades of sales success and executive experience, Jeff provides proven strategies for professionals to face challenges head-on, lead real change, and create thriving sales organizations.

Offering real-world tools and solutions for real estate sales, Jeff's reputation for clarity, humor, authority, and sincerity makes him one of the most requested speakers among businesses and sales and marketing organizations across the United States. Watch Jeff's blend of savvy, substance, and style in action and connect with him online at jeffshore.com.

For more information about booking Jeff, please contact Cassandra Grauer at (530) 558-9109 or email cassandra@jeffshore.com.

ORDER DISCOUNTED MULTIPLE COPIES FOR YOUR SALES TEAM

If you would like to order multiple copies of *The 4:2 Formula* for your sales team, we happily offer bulk discounts. Please contact Cassandra Grauer at (530) 558-9109 or email cassandra@jeffshore.com.